Praise for *The Lost E*

"Conrad Anker and David Roberts combine two riveting tales of discovery: George Mallory's heroic 1924 attempt to reach the summit of Mount Everest, and Anker's discovery of Mallory's body seventy-five years later. . . . *The Lost Explorer* is an exciting glimpse at what some consider the end of The Age of Discovery. Whether Mallory and Irvine reached the summit or not, this book is a lasting tribute to two men whose exploits will continue to fascinate and inspire adventurers."

—Winston Carter, *Chicago Tribune*

"A compelling and authoritative read. Not only did [Anker] discover Mallory, but he made essentially a free climb up the intimidating 'second step' that forms the primary barrier to any north-route climber, and thus shows how Mallory could have conquered the mountain."

—Mike Leary, *Baltimore Sun*

"Immediate and gripping."

—Diane Daniel, *The Boston Globe*

"Coming as it does from a climber of exceptional skill, [Anker's] account has the ring of authenticity."

—John Holkeboer, *The Wall Street Journal*

The
Lost
Explorer

FINDING MALLORY
ON MOUNT EVEREST

Conrad Anker and
David Roberts

A TOUCHSTONE BOOK
PUBLISHED BY SIMON & SCHUSTER
NEW YORK   LONDON   TORONTO   SYDNEY   SINGAPORE

 TOUCHSTONE
Rockefeller Center
1230 Avenue of the Americas
New York, NY 10020

First Touchstone Edition 2001
TOUCHSTONE and colophon are
registered trademarks of Simon & Schuster, Inc.
Designed by Edith Fowler
Line art by Conrad Anker

Manufactured in the United States of America

10 9 8 7 6 5 4 3 2 1

The Library of Congress has cataloged the Simon & Schuster edition
as follows:
Anker, Conrad.
The lost explorer: finding Mallory on Mount Everest / Conrad Anker
and David Roberts.
p. cm.
1. Leigh-Mallory, George Herbert, 1886–1924. 2. Mountaineers—
Great Britan—Biography. 3. Mountaineering—Everest, Mount
(China and Nepal) 4. Anker, Conrad. I. Roberts, David, 1943– II. Title.

GV199.92.L44 A54 1999

99-046131

ISBN 0-684-87151-3
     0-684-87152-1 (Pbk)

Photo Credits:
The Alpine Club Library Collection: 2, 3, 4, 7, 8
Copyright © 1999 by Conrad Anker: 15, 21
Copyright © 1999 by Jake Norton/Mallory & Irvine Research
     Expedition: 18
John Noel/Royal Geographical Society: 6
Copyright 1999 by Thom Pollard: 10 (Photo by S. Scott), 11–14, 16, 17,
     19, 20
Royal Geographical Society: 1, 5
N. E. Odell/Royal Geographical Society: 9
Copyright © 1988 by Galen Rowell/Mountain Light: 18

To the shining memory
of George Leigh Mallory and
Andrew Irvine

Contents

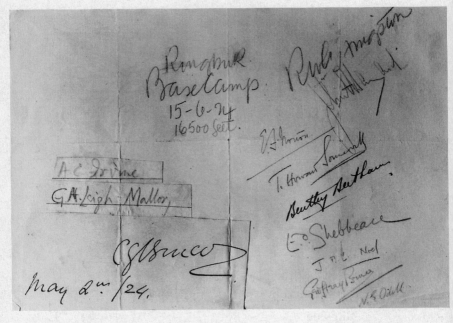

On June 15, the day before leaving Base Camp for home, the surviving members of the 1924 Everest expedition wrote their names on a piece of paper, leaving space on the left for the signatures of the team's ill and absent leader, General Charles Bruce, as well as of the vanished Irvine and Mallory. These were clipped from letters received and notes written on the mountain and pasted in. The original page was later bound into a copy of *The Fight for Everest*, which was published in 1925.
—*Courtesy of the American Alpine Club Library, Golden, Colorado*

Prologue

DR

LIKE MOST CLIMBERS, I grew up steeped in the legend of Mallory and Irvine. Indeed, the long, rich narrative of mountaineering contains no more stirring or enigmatic chapter. As a teenager, clumping up a stony ridge toward the wind-lashed apex of some nondescript peak in my native Colorado, I often conjured up that heroic pair, angling into the sky on June 8, 1924, fighting their way higher than human beings had ever climbed, as they closed in on the summit of Mount Everest.

At that moment, ten days shy of his thirty-eighth birthday, George Leigh Mallory was Britain's finest mountaineer. A man blessed with a preternatural gracefulness, with beauty and charm that dazzled his friends and admirers, he had become obsessed with reaching the highest point on earth. His partner, Andrew "Sandy" Irvine, a relative novice at twenty-two, still an undergraduate at Oxford, had nonetheless proven himself the perfect acolyte in this quest for an alpine grail.

What the leader of the 1924 expedition, on which Mallory and Irvine were lost, wrote afterward rings true today—Mallory was "the greatest antagonist that Everest has had—or is like to have." And Irvine, though destined ever after to languish in the shade of Mallory's fame, remains, in the vignette of another teammate, the epitome of the "natural adept. . . . He could follow, if not lead, anywhere."

At 12:50 on the afternoon of June 8, 1924, climbing solo to 26,000 feet in support of the summit duo, Noel Odell saw the clouds part briefly, giving him a fugitive glimpse of a pair of figures far above him, outlined against the sky, "moving expeditiously" over a steep step of rock and ice on the northeast ridge, less than a thousand feet below the top. This has come down to us as perhaps the most haunting sighting in the annals of exploration. Then the clouds closed in, and Mallory and Irvine vanished into history.

With the sole exception of Amelia Earhart, no lost explorer in the twentieth century has provoked a more intense outpouring of romantic speculation than George Mallory. The question of what happened to him and his young companion, of how those two brave men met their fate, is knotty enough. What spurs the imagination to a higher flight is the possibility that they might have reached Everest's summit before they died—twenty-nine years before Edmund Hillary and Tenzing Norgay made the mountain's official first ascent. If Mallory and Irvine had succeeded, they could have laid fair claim to having pulled off the greatest mountaineering feat ever performed.

Thus the mystery of Mallory and Irvine was handed down to all later generations of climbers. But for me, at age eighteen, the conundrum took on a more personal dimension. As a freshman at Harvard, I drifted into the circle of the university's mountaineering club, which at the time comprised the most accomplished gang of college climbers in the country. Among the six or seven especially talented and flamboyant upperclassmen, who had already notched their belts with such daunting Canadian summits as Logan, Waddington, and Stiletto Needle, one in particular became first my hero, then my mentor, and then my friend and partner.

Scraggly-bearded, soft-spoken, quicksilver smart, slyly iconoclastic, brilliant on vertical rock and ice, absentminded as a dreamy preschooler, Rick Millikan seemed cut from a Viking mold. On an autumn weekend at the Shawangunks, in New York state, Rick dragged me up the hardest and most exhilarating rock pitch I had yet tackled; that January, he broke trail along the frozen crest of New Hampshire's Presidential Range, as I struggled to keep up in a –30° F. gale.

Sometime during that freshman year, I learned that Rick was George Mallory's grandson. Born in 1941, Rick of course had never known his illustrious forebear. His mother, Clare, the eldest of Mallory's three children, had been eight when her father disappeared. She remembered much about him, and she passed down her stories to her three sons.

As Rick and I became good friends, we sometimes talked about Mallory. He believed his grandfather had summitted that June day so long ago; pressed for a rationale, he fell back on intuition. "Those guys were good," he said, if memory serves. "They knew what they were doing up there."

Rick's other grandfather was Robert Millikan, of the famous oil drop experiment, who had won the 1923 Nobel Prize in physics. Clare Mallory had married Robert Millikan's son, Glenn, only to watch, one day in 1947, as her husband was killed as he stood beside her, in a climbing accident in the Great Smoky Mountains of Tennessee. I knew little more about this catastrophe than the bare facts: Rick's father had been hit on the head by a falling stone, in a fluky concatenation of minor miscalculations on a small cliff in the middle of nowhere. He had died instantly. At twenty, I was too shy and awkward to probe further, or to ask Rick to recount the mishap that had cost him his father at an even younger age than Clare had lost hers.

What seemed remarkable, though, was that despite the twin tragedies of her life, Clare had not only tolerated her sons' embrace of this most dangerous sport—she had taught them to climb and heartily encouraged their alpine play. On visits to Berkeley, where Rick had grown up, I got to know Clare, who seemed a classic Edwardian eccentric—a Quaker fiercely devoted to the cause of world peace, a blunt-speaking liberal with no patience for humbug, a true bohemian even in the bohemia of late-1960s Berkeley.

On my first Alaskan expedition, to the Wickersham Wall on Mount McKinley in 1963, Rick and I, with five teammates, were reported missing and feared dead (our bush pilot, poking through storm clouds, had seen our tracks disappear into a chaos of avalanche debris). During the four days we were unaccounted for (we were safely camped far above the avalanche zone), the newspapers interviewed our parents, who gave voice to heartsick fears and hopes against hope. Only Clare was resolutely skeptical, telling the media, in effect, "Nonsense. Those boys know what they're doing."

Three years later, one September afternoon in the Kichatna

Spires, southwest of McKinley, as Rick and I got within forty feet of the summit of an unclimbed, unnamed peak, a big wind slab broke beneath our feet. Helpless to slow our fall, we slid and cartwheeled with the avalanche toward a fatal cliff that loomed below. We had time to anticipate the plunge that lurks, like some dark atavistic memory, in the vulnerable core of the blithest mountaineer's unconscious, before the slide, having carried us 350 feet, miraculously churned to a halt a short distance above the precipice.

I am not sure whether, or how, Rick told his mother about our close call, but the very next summer, he was back with me in Alaska, probing an unexplored range we named the Revelation Mountains. This time Rick's older brother, George, whom I had not climbed with before, came along. (George was even more absentminded than Rick, once in grad school inadvertently locking his professor inside a walk-in bird cage.)

For fifty-two days, we endured the worst weather the Alaska Range could fling at us. Only in recent months have I learned that that summer, for the first time, Clare gave in to the fears that every parent knows. She lost sleep counting the days until we emerged at the end of August, and she extracted a promise from George and Rick that in the Revelations they would never rope up together (better, if it came to that, to lose one son than two).

Of course the brothers Millikan, once on the glacier and out of reach of Mom, promptly disobeyed her. One day George and Rick stormed toward the summit of a beautiful peak we called the Angel, climbing fast along an arête strung with rock towers and ice cliffs. They settled in for the night in a tiny bivouac tent pitched on an airy ledge some 1,000 feet below the top, only to have rain turn to sleet turn to snow whipped by a ferocious wind. Sleepless and hypothermic, they staggered off the mountain the next day, required, in the atrocious conditions—rime ice over slick granite—to rappel almost horizontal pitches. The same storm, 150 miles to the northeast, was in the process of snuffing out the lives of seven trapped climbers among the Wilcox party high on McKinley.

Last May, as the electrifying news that Mallory's body had been discovered on Everest circled the globe, I got in touch with Rick and George and Clare, after a lapse of some years. More than ever, as the details emerged, Rick clung to the belief that before his fatal fall, Mallory had reached the highest point on earth. Clare, now eighty-three, had another sort of interest. "I didn't feel anything much at first," she told me. "I felt that my father's body was far away from his spirit. But I've thought about it more and more in the weeks since. I was anxious to know how he had died. Was it peacefully, as he meditated, or contorted, in pain? I found myself wishing I could be there and comfort him in his pain.

"But all in all, I wish they hadn't found him. I wish they'd left him in peace."

After all these decades, I had felt that in a certain sense I "knew" Mallory myself. But as I researched an article for *National Geographic Adventure* about the discovery, I became acquainted with a man and an explorer even more charismatic, elusive, and remarkable than the mythic figure that had lodged in my head. And as I met and talked to the members of the expedition that had deliberately set out last spring to unravel the mystery of Mallory and Irvine—before the trip, I would have given them about one chance in 10,000 of finding *anything* from the 1924 expedition, let alone Mallory's body—I found a crew of strong, competent, mutually loyal climbers, the kind who do our perilous pastime proud.

Among that crew, however, Conrad Anker stood out. One of the best mountaineers in the world, with an astonishingly varied record of first ascents, Conrad has somehow escaped the megalomania endemic in the world of climbing superstars. He seems instead, at thirty-six, a man firmly grounded in a personal humility; he listens to the cares and needs of others as keenly as to the siren songs of his own ambition; and the Buddhist outlook that draws him toward his Himalayan wanderings has seeped into his spirit, giving him an inner calm. That bedrock stability, that sense of who he is, emerges in the sotto voce notes Conrad occasionally publishes in the *American Alpine Journal*, his only record of some of the boldest climbs ever ventured. His prose in these well-crafted but understated chronicles is like that of a scholar writing judiciously for an audience of his peers.

In the course of our collaboration on this book, I began to realize that, in a certain sense, Conrad Anker was cut from the same cloth as George Mallory. And it became clear that Conrad had an utterly enthralling tale to tell of Everest '99, his own story of Mallory and the mountain.

In this book, then, Conrad and I hope to give voice to the quest of a mountaineer, using all the skills and instincts that half a lifetime of cutting-edge ascents has ingrained in his very fingertips, who last May almost singlehandedly brought back from Everest more insight into the puzzle of Mallory and Irvine than the efforts of seventy-five years of searchers and theorists put together. As we narrate that quest, we also seek, so far as retrospect and judgment allow, to rediscover Mallory himself, the visionary lost explorer whose body Conrad Anker found, and whose fate we may at last begin to divine.

IN THE PAGES THAT FOLLOW, the passages in the first person, dealing primarily with the 1999 expedition, are those of Conrad Anker. The third-person passages, chiefly historical, are by David Roberts.

Snickers and Tea

I HAD JUST SAT DOWN to take off my crampons, because the traverse across the rock band ahead would be easier without them. I drank some fluid—a carbohydrate drink I keep in my water bottle—and sucked a cough drop. At that altitude, it's essential to keep your throat lubricated.

I looked out over this vast expanse. To the south and west, I could see into Nepal, with jagged peaks ranging toward the horizon. In front of me on the north stretched the great Tibetan plateau, brown and corrugated as it dwindled into the distance. The wind was picking up, and small clouds were forming below, on the lee side of some of the smaller peaks.

All of a sudden, a strong feeling came over me that something was going to happen. Something good. I usually feel content when the climb I'm on is going well, but this was different. I felt positive, happy. I was in a good place.

It was 11:45 A.M. on May 1. We were just below 27,000 feet on the north face of Mount Everest. The other four guys were fanned out above me and to the east. They were in sight, but too far away to holler to. We had to use our radios to communicate.

I attached my crampons to my pack, stood up, put the pack on, and started hiking up a small corner. Then, to my left, out of the corner of my eye, I caught a glimpse of a piece of blue and yellow fabric flapping in the wind, tucked behind a boulder. I

thought, I'd better go look at this. Anything that wasn't part of the natural landscape was worth looking at.

When I got to the site, I could see that the fabric was probably a piece of tent that had been ripped loose by the wind and blown down here, where it came to rest in the hollow behind the boulder. It was modern stuff, nylon. I wasn't surprised—there are a lot of abandoned tents on Everest, and the wind just shreds them.

But as I stood there, I carefully scanned the mountain right and left. I was wearing my prescription dark glasses, so I could see really well. As I scanned right, I saw a patch of white, about a hundred feet away. I knew at once there was something unusual about it, because of the color. It wasn't the gleaming white of snow reflecting the sun. It wasn't the white of the chunks of quartzite and calcite that crop up here and there on the north side of Everest. It had a kind of matte look—a light-absorbing quality, like marble.

I walked closer. I immediately saw a bare foot, sticking into the air, heel up, toes pointed downward. At that moment, I knew I had found a human body.

Then, when I got even closer, I could see from the tattered clothing that this wasn't the body of a modern climber. This was somebody very old.

It didn't really sink in at first. It was as if everything was in slow motion. *Is this a dream?* I wondered. *Am I really here?* But I also thought, *This is what we came here to do. This is who we're looking for. This is Sandy Irvine.*

WE'D AGREED BEFOREHAND on a series of coded messages for the search. Everybody on the mountain could listen in on our radio conversations. If we found something, we didn't want some other expedition breaking the news to the world.

"Boulder" was the code word for "body." So I sat down on my pack, got out my radio, and broadcast a message: "Last time I went bouldering in my hobnails, I fell off." It was the first thing that came to mind. I just threw in "hobnails," because an old hobnailed boot—the kind that went out of style way back in the 1940s—was still laced onto the man's right foot. That was another reason I knew he was very old.

We all had our radios stuffed inside our down suits, so it

wasn't easy to hear them. Of the other four guys out searching, only Jake Norton caught any part of my message, and all he heard was "hobnails." I could see him, some fifty yards above me and a ways to the east. Jake sat down, ripped out his radio, and broadcast back, "What was that, Conrad?"

"Come on down," I answered. He was looking at me now, so I started waving the ski stick I always carry at altitude. "Let's get together for Snickers and tea."

Jake knew I'd found something important, but the other three were still oblivious. He tried to wave and yell and get their attention, but it wasn't working. At 27,000 feet, because of oxygen deprivation, you retreat into a kind of personal shell; the rest of the world doesn't seem quite real. So I got back on the radio and put some urgency into my third message: "I'm calling a mandatory group meeting right now!"

Where we were searching was fairly tricky terrain, downsloping shale slabs, some of them covered with a dusting of snow. If you fell in the wrong place, you'd go all the way, 7,000 feet to the Rongbuk Glacier. So it took the other guys a little while to work their way down and over to me.

I rooted through my pack to get out my camera. That morning, at Camp V, I thought I'd stuck it in my pack, but I had two nearly identical stuff sacks, and it turns out I'd grabbed my radio batteries instead. I realized I'd forgotten my camera. I thought, Oh, well, if I had had the camera, I might not have found the body. That's just the way things work.

When I told a friend about this, he asked if I'd read Faulkner's novella *The Bear*. I hadn't. On reading that story, I saw the analogy. The best hunters in the deep Mississippi woods can't even catch a glimpse of Old Ben, the huge, half-mythic bear that has ravaged their livestock for years. It's only when Ike McCaslin gives up everything he's relied on—lays down not only his rifle, but his compass and watch—that, lost in the forest, he's graced with the sudden presence of Old Ben in a clearing: "It did not emerge, appear: it was just there, immobile, fixed in the green and windless noon's hot dappling."

As I sat on my pack waiting for the others, a feeling of awe and respect for the dead man sprawled in front of me started to fill me. He lay face down, head uphill, frozen into the slope. A tuft of hair stuck out from the leather pilot's cap he had on his head. His arms were raised, and his fingers were planted in the scree, as if he'd tried to self-arrest with them. It seemed likely that he was still alive when he had come to rest in this position. There were no gloves on his hands; later I'd think long and hard about the implications of that fact. I took off my own gloves to compare my hands to his. I've got short, thick fingers; his were long and thin, and deeply tanned, probably from the weeks of having walked the track all the way from Darjeeling over the crest of the Himalaya to the north face of Everest.

The winds of the decades had torn most of the clothing away from his back and lower torso. He was naturally mummified—that patch of alabaster I'd spotted from a hundred feet away was the bare, perfectly preserved skin of his back. What was incredible was that I could still see the powerful, well-defined muscles in his shoulders and back, and the blue discoloration of bruises.

Around his shoulders and upper arms, the remnants of seven or eight layers of clothing still covered him—shirts and sweaters and jackets made of wool, cotton, and silk. There was a white, braided cotton rope tied to his waist, about three eighths of an inch in diameter—many times weaker than any rope we'd use today. The rope was tangled around his left shoulder. About ten feet from his waist, I could see the frayed end where the rope had broken. So I knew at once that he'd been tied to his partner, and that he'd taken a long fall. The rope had either broken in the fall, or when his partner tried to belay him over a rock edge.

The right elbow looked as if it was dislocated or broken. It lay imbedded in the scree, bent in an unnatural position. The right scapula was a little disfigured. And above his waist on a right rib, I could see the blue contusion from an upward pull of the rope as it took the shock of the fall.

His right leg was badly broken, both tibia and fibula. With the boot still on, the leg lay at a grotesque angle. They weren't compound fractures—the bones hadn't broken the skin—but they were very bad breaks. My conclusion was that in the fall, the right side of the man's body had taken the worst of the impact. It looked as though perhaps in his last moments, the man had laid his good left leg over his broken right, as if to protect it from further harm. The left boot may have been whipped off in the fall, or it may have eroded and fallen apart. Only the tongue of the boot was present, pinched between the bare toes of his left foot and the heel of his right boot.

Goraks—the big black ravens that haunt the high Himalaya—had pecked away at the right buttock and gouged out a pretty extensive hole, big enough for a gorak to enter. From that orifice, they had eaten out most of the internal organs, simply hollowed out the body.

The muscles of the left lower leg and the thighs had become stringy and desiccated. It's what happens, apparently, to muscles exposed for seventy-five years. The skin had split and opened up, but for some reason the goraks hadn't eaten it.

After fifteen or twenty minutes, Jake Norton arrived. Then the others, one by one: first Tap Richards, then Andy Politz, then Dave Hahn. They didn't say much: just, "Wow, good job, Conrad," or, "This has to be Sandy Irvine." Later Dave said, "I started blinking in awe," and Tap remembered, "I was pretty blown away. It was obviously a body, but it looked like a Greek or Roman marble statue."

The guys took photos, shot some video, and discussed the nuances of the scene. There seemed to be a kind of taboo about touching him. Probably half an hour passed before we got up the nerve to touch him. But we had agreed that if we found Mallory or Irvine, we would perform as professional an excavation as we could under the circumstances, to see if what we found might cast any light on the mystery of their fate. We had even received permission from John Mallory (George's son) to take a small DNA sample.

Tap and Jake did most of the excavating work. We'd planned to cut small squares out of the clothing to take down to Base Camp and analyze. Almost at once, on the collar of one of the shirts, Jake found a name tag. It read, "G. Mallory." Jake looked at us and said, "That's weird. Why would Irvine be wearing Mallory's shirt?"

SOMETIME ON THE MORNING of June 8, 1924, George Mallory and Sandy Irvine set out from Camp VI, at 26,800 feet on the northeast ridge. The day before, the porters who had carried gear and food up to the camp in support of the summit bid brought down a note from Mallory, addressed to the expedition cinematographer, John Noel, who was ensconced at Camp III, more than 5,000 feet below.

> Dear Noel,
>
> We'll probably start early to-morrow (8ᵗʰ) in order to have clear weather. It won't be too early to start looking for us either crossing the rock band under the pyramid or going up skyline at 8.0 p.m.
>
> Yours ever,
> G. Mallory

Noel had a 600 millimeter lens that the expedition members used like a telescope to track their teammates' movements high on Everest. All subsequent commentators have assumed, as Odell did on reading the note, that Mallory's "8.0 p.m." was a slip of the pen, that he meant to write "8:00 A.M." In that case, Mallory's estimate of where he would be was exceedingly optimistic, for it was rare in the era of early Himalayan campaigns for a pair of climbers to get off from any high camp before 6:30 in the morning.

The 1924 expedition was the third of three attempts—all British—on the world's highest mountain; it followed a thoroughgoing reconnaissance in 1921 and a nervy assault the year after. Only Mallory had been a member of all three expeditions. Yet the weather in May 1924 had proved atrocious, defeating a very strong team's best efforts even to put themselves in position for a summit thrust. Later the tea planters in Darjeeling would aver that for at least the previous twenty years, "no such weather had been known at this season."

Then, with the climbers' hopes all but extinguished, the

mountain had laid a spell of grace upon them, giving them day after day of fine weather, although the men woke each morning dreading the onset of the inevitable monsoon, which, normally arriving around June 1, would enfold the Himalaya in a four-month miasma of heavy snow.

As Mallory and Irvine closed their canvas tent and headed along the windswept ridge, they were full of a bursting anticipation. Only four days before, their teammate E. F. "Teddy" Norton, at the end of a gallant effort, had reached 28,126 feet— the highest anyone had ever climbed—before turning back a mere 900 feet below the summit. Norton had made his gutsy push without the aid of bottled oxygen. Mallory and Irvine were breathing gas, and though Mallory had initially been a skeptic about its efficacy, on the 1922 expedition he had learned firsthand that climbers aided by oxygen high on Everest could easily double the climbing speed of those without.

On the 1924 assault, as he had during the two previous expeditions, Mallory had proven himself the strongest and most ambitious climber. By now, his personal obsession with Everest had cranked as tight as it could be wound. In a letter to his wife, Ruth, written six weeks before from Chiblung, on the approach to Everest, he had predicted, "It is almost unthinkable . . . that I shan't get to the top; I can't see myself coming down defeated."

If his twenty-two-year-old companion was daunted by Mallory's hubris, he gave no indication of it. In his diary only four days before his own attempt, awaiting the outcome of Teddy Norton's bold summit bid with teammate Howard Somervell, Irvine had written, "I hope they've got to the top, but by God, I'd like to have a whack at it myself."

Ever since 1924, observers have wondered why Mallory chose Irvine as his partner for the second summit attempt, rather than the far more experienced Noel Odell, who had rounded into incomparable form at high altitude during the preceding week. Irvine had very little climbing experience, with only an exploratory outing in Spitsbergen under his belt. (In a letter to Ruth, Mallory had voiced a qualm, "I wish Irvine had had a season in the Alps.") But on Everest, the Oxford undergraduate had proved to be tougher than several of his more seasoned comrades, an uncomplaining worker, and a delightful companion. He was also something of a mechanical genius, who had taken apart the oxygen apparatus in the field and rebuilt it in a lighter and more efficient form. And since oxygen would be the key to Mallory's all-out dash for the summit, it made sense to have Irvine along.

That day, June 8, 1924, among the rest of the team, only Odell, climbing solo up to Camp VI in support of the summit duo, was high on the mountain. A professional geologist, he had chosen the day to wander in zigzags up the north face, looking for unusual formations. By late morning, he was swimming in a private ecstasy, for there, in one of the most barren places on earth, he had discovered the first fossils ever found on Everest.

At 12:50 in the afternoon, Odell mounted a small crag around 26,000 feet just as the clouds abruptly cleared. Squinting upward, he was treated to the brief vision that has beguiled and tantalized all Everest students since. As Odell later wrote:

> I saw the whole summit ridge and final peak of Everest unveiled. I noticed far away on a snow slope leading up to what seemed to me to be the last step but one from the base of the final pyramid, a tiny object moving and approaching the rock step. A second object followed, and then climbed to the top of the step. . . . I could see that they were moving expeditiously as if endeavouring to make up for lost time.

Then the clouds closed over the scene. Odell climbed on to Camp VI, where he found, to his mild alarm, pieces of oxygen equipment strewn about the tent, suggesting that Irvine had perhaps made some desperate last-minute adjustment to the apparatus. And Odell was disturbed that he had seen his pair of friends still well below the summit pyramid at almost 1:00 P.M., or five hours after Mallory's blithe prediction. An afternoon snow squall cleared, but now Odell could see no signs of human presence on the upper ridge, bathed in warm sunlight. He scrambled some 200 feet above the camp, whistling and yodeling in case Mallory and Irvine should be nearing it on their descent. Then, with a heavy heart, Odell headed down the mountain, as Mallory had ordered him to, for the small tent at Camp VI could not hold three climbers.

During the next two days, in an astonishing performance,

Odell climbed first to Camp V, then alone all the way back up to Camp VI. When he found the tent exactly as he had left it on June 8, he knew the worst. He laid two sleeping bags in the snow in a figure T—the prearranged signal to a teammate watching below that all hope was lost.

DURING THE SEVENTY-FIVE YEARS after the 1924 expedition retreated from the mountain, only two further pieces of hard information cast any light on the mystery of Mallory and Irvine's fate, but each was as tantalizing as Odell's vision of the twin figures outlined against the sky. In 1933, on the first expedition to Everest after Mallory's, Percy Wyn Harris found an ice axe lying on a rock slab, 250 yards short of what had come to be called the First Step—thus considerably below where the pair had been at the time of Odell's 12:50 sighting. Plainly the axe belonged to either Mallory or Irvine, but as a piece of evidence, it was maddeningly ambiguous. Had one of the climbers dropped it during the ascent? Or had it been deliberately laid aside, as unnecessary on the mostly rocky terrain that stretched above? Or, more ominously, did it mark the site of a fatal accident on the descent, as one man dropped the axe to make a futile effort to belay his falling partner?

From 1938, the year of the last British prewar expedition, to 1960, when a Chinese team claimed to make the first ascent of Everest from the north, the Tibetan side of the mountain went virtually unvisited. It was not until 1979 that China first granted permission to foreigners to approach the mountain through its "province" of Tibet. That year, the second tantalizing clue to Mallory and Irvine's demise came to light.

The climbing leader of a Sino-Japanese expedition, Ryoten Hasegawa, had a provocative conversation with one of its Chinese members, Wang Hongbao. Wang told Hasegawa that four years earlier, in 1975, during the second Chinese attack on Everest, he had gone out for a short walk from Camp VI, near 27,000 feet. Within twenty minutes of leaving his tent, he had come across the body of a fallen climber. It was, he insisted, "an old English dead." The man's clothes had turned to dust and blown away in the winds of the decades. He was lying on his side, and one of his cheeks had been pecked away by goraks.

Between Hasegawa's Japanese and Wang's Chinese, the conversation took place in a linguistic muddle. Hasegawa wondered whether the dead man could have been a Russian from a long-rumored (and now debunked) secret 1952 attempt, on which six climbers were supposed to have died; but Wang vigorously demurred, repeating "English, English!"

Hasegawa realized that the body might well have been that of Mallory or Irvine. But before he could question Wang further, only a day after sharing his startling confidence, the Chinese climber died when he was avalanched into a crevasse, leaving a profound enigma in his wake.

During the last two decades, scores of expeditions have attacked Everest from the north. All of them have kept their eyes peeled for any further sign of the lost climbers, to no avail. An American mountaineer-historian, Tom Holzel, became obsessed with the puzzle, and after extensive research and inquiry, narrowed down the area of search to a large quadrangle on the north face, below the ridge route Mallory and Irvine had essayed. In 1986, Holzel organized the first expedition with the goal of systematically searching for the vanished pair. The team included such first-rate climbers as David Breashears, Sue Giller, and Dave Cheesmond, but terrible weather thwarted their efforts to go higher than 26,100 feet—nearly a thousand feet below Holzel's search zone. (In retrospect, it would become clear that a search in the autumn season, such as the 1986 team conducted, was doomed to failure because of the vast quantities of snow the summer-long monsoon inevitably dumps.)

Before the expedition, Holzel had synthesized all his research in a house-of-cards hypothesis that he laid out in the concluding chapter of *First on Everest: The Mystery of Mallory & Irvine* (co-authored with Audrey Salkeld). According to Holzel, Mallory and Irvine faced the realization that they would run out of bottled oxygen well below the summit. Mallory was, in Holzel's view, the stronger climber, Irvine perhaps intimidated by a challenge well beyond any he had previously faced. In any event, Irvine gave his remaining gas to his partner, then descended as Mallory headed solo for the summit.

Carried away by his own theorizing, Holzel wrote as if recording solid history, not educated guess:

Splitting up at 1 P.M., Mallory quickly raced up the final pyramid of Everest's summit. Irvine returned past the First Step and started his descending traverse of the North Face slabs. . . . Perhaps after numerous small slips, each caught in time, Irvine lost control as both his feet shot out from under him. Turning to catch himself with his ice axe, it wrenched out of his exhausted grip. He tumbled 1,000 feet to the snow terrace below.

Holzel was further convinced that Mallory reached the summit, only to die of hypothermia in the bivouac he could not have avoided, or in a fall, perhaps all the way to the Rongbuk Glacier.

In the years after 1986, most informed observers questioned Holzel's assertion that Mallory had made the summit. But the notion of the two climbers splitting up, with Irvine dropping his axe and slipping to his death on the north face, came to be a kind of received wisdom. The body that Wang Hongbao had found near Camp VI, then, had to be Irvine's. It was for this reason that all five searchers last May, as they stared at the "marble statue" lying frozen face down in the scree, assumed they were looking at Sandy Irvine.

To settle for good the all-important question of whether Mallory and/or Irvine reached the summit in 1924, only two possibilities loom. The first is that some relic—a piece of gear, a keepsake, or a note unmistakably belonging to one of the men—might be found on or near the top. But the hundreds of successful summitteers over the last forty-six years have never found anything of that kind. (Looking for traces of predecessors in 1953, Edmund Hillary peered down the north ridge and declared it unclimbable.)

The other possibility touches on the kind of wild surmise normally found only in the pages of Conan Doyle. We know that Mallory carried a Kodak Vestpocket camera. If the camera could be found, and the film, deep-frozen since 1924, could be developed, a photo clearly taken from the summit—an image of such mountains as Ama Dablam or Lhotse, for instance, invisible from anywhere on Everest's north face—would clinch the case. (In 1897, a three-man Swedish expedition led by Salomon Andrée, attempting to balloon to the North Pole, vanished in the Arctic. Thirty-three years later, the men's bodies were

found on remote White Island. The pictures in the men's camera, perfectly preserved, delivered a vivid testament to the trio's
last days and to the mishaps that doomed them.)

During the last few years, a young German graduate student in geology has taken up the quest where Tom Holzel left
off. Jochen Hemmleb, twenty-seven, is a climber of modest abilities, but a researcher whose obsession with detail puts even
Holzel's in the shade. A self-professed disciple of the English
writer Audrey Salkeld (who is the world's leading authority on
Mallory), Hemmleb became fascinated with the 1924 saga.
From a single, mediocre photo published in a quirky book celebrating the 1975 Chinese expedition, Hemmleb figured out that
that year's Camp VI had been pitched in an entirely different
place from nearly all other expeditions' Camp VI. Studying
background details, Hemmleb thought he could extrapolate the
likely location of the fugitive camp. A search, then, for the body
Wang Hongbao had found ought to focus on all terrain within a
plausible twenty-minute stroll of that camp.

In 1998, Hemmleb got in touch with Mount Rainier guide
Eric Simonson, who had climbed Everest from the north in
1991. Soon infected with the German's enthusiasm, Simonson
put together a climbing team and a network of sponsors. Most
of his teammates were fellow Rainier guides, but at the last moment, he snagged a genuine star in Conrad Anker, whose record
of cutting-edge first ascents on remote mountains ranging from
Patagonia to the Karakoram can be matched by only two or
three other Americans. The BBC and *NOVA* agreed to co-
produce a film about the expedition, and a Seattle-based Web
site, MountainZone, signed on to cover the team via daily Internet dispatches from Base Camp.

Most observers, however, viewed the expedition as something of a boondoggle—one more stratagem, like campaigns to
raise money for medical research or to clean up other expeditions' trash, to finance an expensive outing on the world's
highest mountain. Even if Simonson and Hemmleb's mo-
tives were sincere, after all the expeditions that had crisscrossed
the northern slopes of Everest over the years, the chances of
finding something new from the 1924 expedition seemed infin-
itesimal.

Anker himself, in the middle of a month-long jaunt among

unclimbed towers in Antarctica in 1997, had vocally derided the Everest circuses of recent years. In March 1999, on the eve of his departure for Nepal, one of Anker's friends invited him to dinner.

"What are you up to, Conrad?" the friend asked over coffee.

"I'm off for Tibet. A little high-altitude trekking."

"Kailas?" The friend named the famous holy mountain, object of Buddhist and Hindu pilgrimages.

"No, a little higher," said Anker sheepishly. "I'm going to Everest."

OUR FIRST PRIORITY was to look for traces of Mallory and Irvine. Most of the guys wanted to go to the summit, but Eric Simonson—"Simo," as we call him—emphasized that the search was the primary reason we had come to Everest.

It wasn't until April 30 that we had camps in place and ropes fixed and were ready to conduct the search. Fixing ropes entails securing small-diameter cords most of the way up the route; these ropes, left in place throughout the expedition, serve as safety lines and make both ascent and descent quicker and easier.

One thing that gave us a lot of hope was that the snowfall the previous winter had been extraordinarily light. Even peering out the windows of our jet as we flew into Kathmandu, we could see that the mountain was as bare as it ever gets. When we reached Base Camp, Simo, who'd been on six previous Everest expeditions, couldn't believe the conditions—the mountain was the driest it had been in living memory. And all through April, we got really good weather. If ever a season was ideal for a search, it was in the spring of 1999.

At 5:15 on the morning of May 1, just as it was getting light, the five of us—Andy Politz, Tap Richards, Jake Norton, Dave Hahn, and I—headed out from Camp V, at 25,600 feet. There was a pretty stiff wind, and most of the going in the early hours was in the shade, so it was quite cold. We followed the regular route up to Camp VI, at 27,000 feet, getting there about 10:30.

I'd decided not to use oxygen. I wanted to know how my body would perform at that altitude. Dave, whom I'd climbed with in Antarctica, was a little upset with me. He thought I'd be more efficient if I was sucking gas. But as it was, I got to Camp VI before he did. So he said, "Well, I guess you don't need that stuff."

Dave and Andy had both climbed Everest before from the north. Andy had been on the mountain four previous times. But I'd never been this high before. The highest I'd ever been was 24,000 feet, on an unsuccessful expedition to Annapurna IV. The highest summit I'd reached was Latok II, in the Karakoram, about 23,300 feet.

From Camp VI, we started traversing to the right, or west, toward the search zone that Jochen Hemmleb had identified. He had made a circle on the map that covered all the ground he thought was within a likely twenty-minute walk of where he thought the Chinese Camp VI had been in 1975. Simo estimated the size of that area as equal to twelve football fields. There was no way the five of us could completely cover that ground in one day. I actually thought of what we were undertaking as a kind of reconnaissance. As we headed out there, I thought, It's just good that we're here to look. No one has ever searched this high before.

Jochen had given us what he called the "research manual"—it was an eight-page, spiral-bound, laminated notebook telling us how, why, and where to search. Initially we had all these grand ideas about how we'd cover the ground. We'd hike to a high point, spread twenty yards apart, and head downhill. But when you get to 27,000 feet, you're in a different world. Your mind needs oxygen to work, and there isn't much oxygen up there.

Pretty early Jake found an oxygen bottle with blue paint on one end. He got on the radio to Jochen at Base Camp and described the cylinder, and Jochen was able to verify that it was a Chinese '75 bottle. So we knew we were in the right vicinity.

Meanwhile I'd started to drift out of earshot of the others, lower and farther right. Jochen had located the Chinese Camp

VI higher than I thought it was likely to have been. I was using my mountaineer's intuition, not the research manual. I thought, Now where would I pitch a camp on this part of the mountain? I was coming at it fresh—I hadn't overanalyzed, projecting preconceived "facts" onto reality.

Also, I was skeptical about the "twenty-minute stroll." Your sense of time at altitude goes haywire. You can say, "Okay, I'll see you in forty-five minutes," but up there you don't even realize how time slips away. And there was another question—just how strong was Wang Hongbao? Some of his Tibetan teammates could really cruise at 27,000 feet. Who knows how far Wang might have gone in twenty minutes?

I walked down and right, over a little crest of an ill-defined rib. Then, about 11:00 A.M., looking down, I saw the first body. He had on a purple suit. I walked up closer to check him out. He was lying head downhill, almost hidden on the downhill side of a rock. His legs were obviously broken or dislocated. He was pretty beat up—he'd taken a long fall. His right arm was stuck straight out, as though he were waving. We would later nickname him "the Greeter." With his plastic boots and metal ascender, he was obviously modern.

The goraks had eaten away his face. There was just the skull. It was very macabre.

I realized right away that the Greeter wasn't who we were looking for; but all the same, there was a lot of information there. One of his boots was off. I think that's common—when people really accelerate in a fall, the boots can get whipped off, because you don't lace them too tight at altitude, for fear of cutting off circulation. And it was significant that his head was downhill. I'd had several informal chats with other mountaineers, asking them what the dead bodies they had found on mountains all over the world looked like. Almost invariably, the head was downhill. Why that might be, I'm not sure. Perhaps the upper torso and head are denser than the rest of the body, and if you carry a pack, that makes you even more top-heavy.

As I looked at the Greeter, I realized I was in a natural catchment basin. I asked myself, Why did he stop right here, on the downhill side of this rock? The ridge I was on had a lot of rock snags and outcroppings, places where a body would naturally come to rest. It's like a river, with eddies downstream from boulders. Or avalanches in winter, which I've been studying as long as I've been climbing—how they take out certain trees and don't take out certain other ones, according to their run-out tracks and deposition zones. There's no way to analyze all the forces on a mountain rationally; it has to be intuitive. The more experience you have, the more you absorb on a subconscious level.

So I kept traversing right, exploring this catchment basin. In the back of my mind, I wanted to look into the Great Couloir, which is way beyond Jochen's search zone. I wanted to see the route by which Reinhold Messner had made his astounding solo, oxygenless ascent of Everest in 1980. On this standard-setting climb, Messner had to scale, 250 yards farther west, the same cliff bands that form the Second Step. How had he unlocked the north face? My curiosity drew me westward.

By now my partners were still in sight, but they were tiny—they were at least 500 yards away. About 11:30, Andy came on the radio. He said, "Conrad, what are you doing way out there? We need to be more systematic."

I answered, "I'm just looking around. I want to see what this is all about." Even as Andy was talking to me, I'd spotted another body, a fair distance away, a hundred feet below. This guy had on a blue suit so faded it looked gray. Almost all the color had gone out of the fabric, so I was thinking, He could be really old. He could be it.

So I down-climbed to the body. He'd come to rest on the last terrace before a big cliff band. As I got close, I saw that he had on orange overboots with clip-on crampons, so I knew he was modern too. Again, he was lying head downhill, folded in half, his arms and legs at unnatural angles, as if he'd cartwheeled a long, violent way, like a rag doll. I couldn't see his face.

The second body made it all the more obvious that I was in a catchment basin. Looking up the slope, I could see how the natural forces of the mountain had moved the bodies. Now I started traversing back east toward the other guys, along the top of this cliff band. It was steep enough so that if I fell, I wouldn't be able to self-arrest, but it was terrain I felt at home on. Sort of four-wheel-drive scrambling.

Then I sat down to take off my crampons, hydrate, and suck a cough drop. As I started off again, within a couple of paces I caught sight of the shreds of blue and yellow fabric. And then, scanning right, that patch of alabaster. The body that wasn't modern.

WE DIDN'T HAVE all that much time to work. We'd agreed on a tentative turnaround hour of 2:00 P.M., to get back to Camp V while it was still daylight, and by the time we started excavating, it was past noon. There were clouds below us, but only a slight wind. As one can imagine, this was hard work at 26,700 feet (the altitude of the body, as I later calculated it). We had taken off our oxygen gear, because it was just too cumbersome to dig with it on.

Because the body was frozen into the scree, we had to chip away at the surrounding ice and rock with our ice axes. It took some vigorous swings even to dislodge little chunks, the ice was so dense. We were all experienced climbers, we were used to swinging tools, so we did the chipping pretty efficiently; only once did a pick glance off a rock and impale the man's arm. As we got closer to the body, we put down our axes and started chipping with our pocketknives.

We were so sure this was Sandy Irvine that Jake actually sat down, took a smooth piece of shale in his lap, and started to scratch out a tombstone with Irvine's name and dates, 1902–1924. But then we found the "G. Mallory" tag on the collar, and shortly after, Tap found another one on a seam under the arm. It read, "G. Leigh Mallory." We just stared at each other, stunned, as we realized this wasn't Irvine. We had found George Mallory.

As we excavated, Tap chipped away on his left side, Jake on his right. I did mostly lifting and prying. Dave and Andy took pictures and shot video.

It was good fortune that George was lying on his stomach, because most of the stuff you carry when you climb is in the front pockets, so it had been protected by his body for seventy-five years. It may seem funny, or even pretentious, but we referred to him as "George," not as "Mallory." All through the weeks before, we'd talked about Mallory and Irvine so much that it was as if we knew them, like old friends; they had become George and Sandy.

We left George's face where it was, frozen into the scree,

but once I could lift the lower part of his body, Tap and Jake could reach underneath him and go through the pockets. The body was like a frozen log. When I lifted it, it made that same creaky noise as when you pull up a log that's been on the ground for years.

It was disconcerting to look into the hole in the right buttock that the goraks had chewed. His body had been hollowed out, almost like a pumpkin. You could see the remains of seeds and some other food—very possibly Mallory's last meal.

We didn't go near George's head. We moved the loose rock away from it, but we didn't try to dig it out. I think that was a sort of unspoken agreement, and at the time, none of us wanted to look at his face.

Of course we were most excited about the possibility of finding the camera. Jake even thought for a minute he'd found it. George had a small bag that was lodged under his right biceps. Jake reached in there, squeezed the bag, and felt a small, square object, just about the right size. We finally had to cut the bag to get the object out, and when we did, we found it wasn't the camera after all, it was a tin of beef lozenges!

The clincher that it was Mallory came when Jake pulled out a neatly folded, new-looking silk handkerchief in which several letters had been carefully wrapped. They were addressed to Mallory. On the envelope of one of them, for instance, we read, "George Leigh Mallory Esq., c/o British Trade Agent, Yalung Tibet."

Besides the letters, we found a few penciled notes in other pockets. As we found out later, they were all about logistics, about bringing so many loads to Camp VI, and so on. We read them carefully, hoping Mallory might have jotted down a note about reaching the summit or turning back, but there was nothing of the sort.

One by one, Jake and Tap produced what we started calling "the artifacts." It seemed an odd collection of items to carry to the summit of Everest. There was a small penknife; a tiny pencil, about two and a half inches long, onto which some kind of mint cake had congealed (we could still smell the mint); a needle and thread; a small pair of scissors with a file built into one blade; a second handkerchief, well used (the one he blew his nose on), woven in a red and yellow floral pattern on a blue background, with the monogram G.L.M. in yellow; a box of special matches, Swan Vestas, with extra phosphorus on the tips; a little piece of leather with a hose clamp on it that might have been a mouthpiece for the oxygen apparatus; a tube of zinc oxide, rolled partway up; a spare pair of fingerless mittens that looked like they hadn't been used.

Two other artifacts seemed particularly intriguing. Jake found a smashed altimeter in one pocket. The hand was missing from the dial, but you could see that the instrument had been specially calibrated for Everest, with a range from 20,000 feet to 30,000 feet. Inscribed on the back, in fine script, was "M.E.E. II"—for Mount Everest Expedition II. And in the vest pocket, we found a pair of goggles. The frames were bent, but the green glass was unbroken. It was Andy who came up with the possible significance of the goggles being in the pocket. To him, it argued that George had fallen after dusk. If it had been in the daytime, he would have been wearing the goggles, even on rock. He'd just had a vivid lesson in the consequences of taking them off during the day, when Teddy Norton got a terrible attack of snow blindness the night after his summit push on June 4.

As we removed each artifact, we put it carefully in a Ziploc bag. Andy volunteered to carry the objects down to Camp V. To some people, it may seem that taking George's belongings with us was a violation. We even had a certain sense that we were disturbing the dead—I think that's why we had hesitated to begin the excavation. But this was the explicit purpose of the expedition: to find Mallory and Irvine and to retrieve the artifacts and try to solve the mystery of what had happened on June 8, 1924. I think we did the right thing.

As interesting as what we found was what we didn't find. George had no backpack on, nor any trace of the frame that held the twin oxygen bottles. His only carrying sack was the little bag we found under his right biceps. He didn't have any water bottle, or Thermos flask, which was what they used in '24. He didn't have a flashlight, because he'd forgotten to take it with him. We know this not from Odell, but from the 1933 party, who found the flashlight in the tent at the 1924 Camp VI.

And we didn't find the camera. That was the great disappointment.

It was getting late—we'd already well overstayed our 2:00

P.M. turnaround. The last thing we gathered was a DNA sample, to analyze for absolute proof of the identity of the man we'd found. Simonson had received approval for this procedure beforehand from John Mallory, George's only son, who's seventy-nine and living in South Africa. I had agreed to do this job.

I cut an inch-and-a-half-square patch of skin off the right forearm. It wasn't easy. I had to use the serrated blade on Dave's utility knife. Cutting George's skin was like cutting saddle leather, cured and hard.

Since the expedition, I've often wondered whether taking the tissue was a sacrilegious act. In Base Camp, I had volunteered for the task. On the mountain, I had no time to reflect whether or not this was the right thing to do.

We wanted to bury George, or at least to cover him up. There were rocks lying around, but not a lot that weren't frozen in place. We formed a kind of bucket brigade, passing rocks down to the site.

Then Andy read, as a prayer of committal, Psalm 103: "As for man, his days are as grass: as a flower of the field, so he flourisheth./For the wind passeth over it, and it is gone . . ."

We finally left at 4:00 P.M. I lingered a bit after the other four. The last thing I did was to leave a small Butterfinger candy bar in the rocks nearby, like a Buddhist offering. I said a sort of prayer for him, several times over.

The other guys traversed back to Camp VI to rejoin the normal route down to V, but I saw that I could take a shortcut and go straight to V. I got there at 5:00 P.M., the others forty-five minutes to an hour later.

Dave and Andy were in one tent, Tap, Jake, and I in the other. Dave said later that it was only back in Camp V that what we'd done really began to sink in, that his emotions spilled out, that he was filled with satisfaction and amazement.

We had some food and tried to sleep. I was pretty tired—it had been a twelve-hour day. I slept soundly for a couple of hours, then I woke up. I was on the downhill side of the tent, getting forced out of the good spot. The wind kept blowing. The rest of the night, I couldn't sleep. Just kept tossing and turning. It was miserable.

In my sleeplessness, I kept reviewing the day. Despite the broken leg and the gorak damage, at George's side I had experienced a powerful feeling that he was at peace with himself. As I had sat next to him, I thought, This man was a fellow climber. We shared the same goals and aspirations, the same joys and sorrows. Our lives were motivated by the same elemental force. When I thought of what a valiant effort George had made, to climb this high on the north side of Everest in 1924, given the equipment and clothing of his day, I was flooded with a sense of awe.

And already, my mind was turning over the implications of what we had found. It seemed unlikely that it was Mallory whose body Wang Hongbao had discovered in 1975. His description—of a man lying on his side, with one cheek pecked out by goraks—was too different from what we had seen. So if Wang had found Irvine, where was he? Did the broken rope mean that the two men had fallen together? In that case, was Irvine's body nearby? And what were the chances that the camera lay with Irvine? Already I was anticipating our second search.

I knew we'd made a major find, but the full impact of it didn't hit me until we went on down the mountain. Despite our radio silence and our cryptic coded messages to each other, by the time we reached Base Camp two days later, the whole world was buzzing with the news that we'd discovered George Mallory.

Mon Dieu!—George Mallory!

DR

IT MIGHT BE ARGUED that in disappearing into the clouds that June day seventy-five years ago, Mallory and Irvine performed the most perfect vanishing act in exploring history. The question of what went wrong to cause their deaths is, in the long run, secondary. Even in the 1990s, it is all too easy to fall off those loose, downward-sloping slabs—like roof tiles, in the words of Teddy Norton—on the north face of Everest, and just as easy to freeze to death in an unplanned bivouac on one of its high, storm-swept ledges. Nor is it particularly surprising that the two men's bodies should have been lost for so many years. Over the decades, any number of stellar mountaineers have disappeared on Everest—among them the British climbers Mick Burke, Pete Boardman, and Joe Tasker, as well as four stalwart Czechs in 1988 who, having made a daring, fast ascent of the southwest face, were never seen or heard from again after making an exhausted last radio call. Despite all the climbers who yearly swarm onto Everest, the mountain is huge enough to hide many secrets, and the glaciers that carry away everything that falls from its slopes have sealed many a hapless mountaineer in an icy tomb.

The conundrum that elevates Mallory and Irvine's vanishing to the realm of the mythic is the possibility that the pair could have reached the summit before they died. Over the years, pressed to pin down exactly where he had seen his friends moving fast along the ridge at 12:50 on June 8, Noel

Odell vacillated. A skeptical man by nature, he allowed other skeptics to convince him that in all likelihood he had seen Mallory and Irvine climbing up the relatively easy First Step, more than 1,000 feet below the top. Yet in his original diary entry, which presumably noted his fresh first perception, Odell wrote, "At 12:50 saw M & I on ridge nearing base of final pyramid"— in other words, less than 500 feet below the summit.

None of the fourteen peaks in the world surpassing 8,000 meters (about 26,240 feet) would be climbed for another twenty-six years, until the French ascent of Annapurna in 1950. This, despite a dozen bold attacks on K2, Kangchenjunga, Nanga Parbat, and Everest in the 1930s, by teams loaded with top-notch American, English, and German mountaineers. If Mallory and Irvine summitted in 1924, their deed stands unique in mountaineering history.

Beyond all this, Mallory himself was one of the most talented, charismatic, and at the same time enigmatic figures ever to cross the stage of mountain conquest. He was born in Cheshire on June 18, 1886, a parson's son. He attended Winchester public school, then went up to Magdalene College, Cambridge. As a child, his sister Avie recalled, "He climbed everything that it was at all possible to climb. I learnt very early that it was fatal to tell him that any tree was impossible for him to get up. 'Impossible' was a word that acted as a challenge to him."

Once, at age seven, George was sent to his room for behaving badly during teatime, only to have his nonplussed family discover him climbing the roof of the adjoining church. "I *did* go to my room," he rationalized with the impudence of youth—"to fetch my cap."

The letters George faithfully wrote his mother during his teenage years brim with boyish high spirits, and with a cocky self-confidence, as he unabashedly narrates his triumphs. For a while, his favorite epithet was "perfectly ripping": "The Grand Combin is 14,100 feet, and of course the view from the top was perfectly ripping."

Bright, charming, and restless, Mallory was inclined at Winchester toward a certain scholastic laziness. Wrote one of his tutors, "Mallory was just a very attractive, natural boy, not a hard worker and behind rather than in front of his contemporaries . . . in intellectual attainments." At Winchester he excelled in football (i.e., soccer) and gymnastics, and "did not like to lose." At Cambridge, he became captain of the Magdalene Boat Club and rowed in the Henley Regatta.

But it was not until the age of eighteen, during the summer before his last year at Winchester, that Mallory first did any real mountaineering, when a tutor, R. L. G. Irving, took him and another student to the Alps. The climbs Irving dragged his novices up were surprisingly ambitious, and during those arduous outings on Monte Rosa and Mont Blanc, Mallory discovered the passion that would center his life.

From his first years onward, two characteristics emerged that would ultimately bear on his fate on Mount Everest. Mallory had a kind of addiction to risk that skeptical observers considered simple recklessness. His sister remembered him telling her that in theory a boy ought to be able to lie on the railroad tracks and escape unharmed as a train ran over him. A characteristic childhood stunt at the beach is recounted by David Robertson, Mallory's definitive biographer:

> One day George went out and perched atop a rough rock, meaning to stay until the incoming tide had surrounded it; he felt quite confident that the tide would turn before the waves touched his feet. On hearing what George was up to, the family hastened to the shore; they could see him very easily, clad in the bright blazer of his first preparatory school. The high spring tide had already cut him off and would soon cover the rock. Grandmother Jebb begged someone to bring the boy in, and with considerable difficulty a young bystander did so. George himself remained quite confident and calm.

Obviously, such a penchant for self-testing was useful in developing the daring apprentice climber George became at eighteen. Some years later, after Mallory had led a very experienced Austrian mountaineer up a difficult route in Wales, the visitor marveled at Mallory's "mastery of the hardest pitches," but inveighed, "That young man will not be alive for long."

The other characteristic was a congenital absentmindedness. There is a famous route on Lliwedd, the great peak in Wales, of which legend has it Mallory made the first ascent, solo at dusk, to recover a pipe he had left on a high ledge that he had reached earlier in the day by a more conventional but less direct itinerary. Even in 1922, on Everest, the expedition leader, General Charles Bruce, in a confidential summary, described Mallory as "a great dear but forgets his boots on all occasions." According to mountain historian Audrey Salkeld, "Forgetting to tie on [to the climbing rope] was a clear demonstration of Mallory's chronic absent-mindedness, a fault he never managed to overcome." On top of his forgetfulness, Mallory had a mechanical ineptitude so extreme he had trouble making his camp stove work.

From adolescence on, Mallory was possessed of an extraordinary beauty. Irving, his first mountain mentor, remembered him at eighteen as "extremely good-looking, with a gentleness about the features, and a smoothness of skin that might suggest effeminacy to a stranger; it never did to a friend." The photos capture Mallory's handsomeness, but no photo could convey the charm and magnetism that made both men and women fall in love with him, often at first sight.

In adulthood, Mallory stood five feet eleven and weighed 159 pounds. His "strikingly beautiful" face was likened by Irving to that of "a Botticelli Madonna." At Cambridge, his tutor, Arthur Benson, twenty-five years Mallory's elder, was hopelessly smitten with the student. In a diary published posthumously, Benson recorded his feelings after a walk with Mallory: "Why should I pretend that I do not love this young friend, and take deep pleasure in his company[?]" Earlier, he had written, "It is a pleasure to me to see him move, or do anything."

At Cambridge, Mallory entered his social element. One of his first climbing companions, Cottie Sanders—better known by her novelist nom de plume, Ann Bridge—testified to the intensity of friendship that Mallory and some of his classmates practiced:

> They held personal relationships as so important that they held only a few other things as being of any importance whatever. . . . They enjoyed each other furiously; delightedly, they examined and explored every means of knowing people better and liking them more. . . . They brought their whole intellectual energy to bear on their

relationships; they wanted to know not only that they loved people but how and why they loved them.

The climate of Cambridge (and of Oxford) in the first decade of our century was a far cry from what we think of as stuffy and Victorian. The whole university was suffused in an atmosphere of idealized love among men—even between men two or three decades apart in age—that owed much to Plato's *Symposium*. There was a freedom within this ideal that few universities in the 1990s would tolerate. Arthur Benson could go for a long walk and picnic with his student, even bathing in the nude, without raising an administrative eyebrow.

To call this climate homosexual is to oversimplify it. Much of Mallory's charisma derived from the fact that he bore the adulation and platonic love of his admirers with a kind of unaffected innocence. As Benson wrote after Mallory's death:

> This was, I think, the essence of his wonderful charm, that he was so unconscious of his great personal beauty, his gifts, and his achievements, while his sympathy with those with whom he came in contact, their tastes, their preferences, their opinions, was deep and genuine.

At Cambridge, though mountaineering was his abiding passion, Mallory threw himself into theater, music, and painting (he became a fervent partisan of the Postimpressionists); he even took, according to his first biographer, David Pye, who was a schoolmate, "to dressing rather peculiarly in black flannel shirts and coloured ties; and grew his hair long."

Pye was also struck by Mallory's contentiousness: "A most persistent and even derisive arguer, he was apt to express himself disdainfully and contemptuously, and to shift his ground, but more because he had not got the issue clear in his mind than from mental agility."

Mallory's impatience, which would become famous, went hand in hand with his apparent recklessness and his verve. According to Pye, "In conversation he was not always easy to follow; he talked so rapidly, and so many words got their wings clipped in the process, as to make him at times almost unintelligible."

At Cambridge, and later in many a Welsh lake, Mallory indulged in a passion for nude bathing. One hot evening, out rowing with schoolmates on the Cam, he stripped down and dived in. When he refused to return to the boat, his friends, fearful of missing the 10:00 P.M. curfew, rowed off and left him. Stark naked, Mallory slunk back to Magdalene College, hoping to climb in an open window, only to be apprehended by a dubious policeman.

Through fellow students James Strachey and Geoffrey Keynes, Mallory drifted within the orbit of that brilliant collection of eccentric bohemian artists and writers known as Bloomsbury. On first beholding this "Greek god," the more unabashed flouters of convention within that circle could hardly contain their rapture. Wrote Lytton Strachey (James's older brother), the mordant biographer of Queen Victoria and other eminent Victorians, to Clive and Vanessa Bell, after his first meeting with Mallory:

> Mon dieu!—George Mallory!—When that's been written, what more need be said? My hand trembles, my heart palpitates, my whole being swoons at the words— oh heavens! heavens! . . . [H]e's six foot high, with the body of an athlete by Praxiteles, and a face—oh incredible—the mystery of Botticelli, the refinement and delicacy of a Chinese print, the youth and piquancy of an unimaginable English boy.

Strachey raved on, in this manner, about spending "hours every day lost in a trance of adoration, innocence, and bliss" after meeting Mallory; stunned by the vision of such youthful beauty, he could, he claimed, "curl up within its shadow, and sleep." Perhaps to mitigate his crush, he added, "For the rest, he's going to be a schoolmaster, and his intelligence is not remarkable. What's the need?"

Strachey's friend the openly homosexual painter Duncan Grant several times persuaded Mallory to pose for him in the nude, and Grant later told Strachey that he would have paid the young man £100 a year to have him as his "mistress." Grant and Strachey regularly compared notes about their young idol.

Strachey insisted that "I'm not in love with him," yet in the next breath gushed,

> But, oh heavens! his body!—the supreme beauty of the face has I'm afraid gone—that wonderful bloom—but it's still intensely attractive, with the eyes, and the colour, and the charming expression, and the strange divine ears, so large and lascivious—oh!!

Just as he sneered at Mallory's interest in schoolteaching, the bookish, ungainly Strachey had no use for what he called "imbecile mountains." After an uncharacteristic jaunt among the Black Cuillins on the Isle of Skye—prime training ground for several generations of British climbers—Strachey dismissed the mountains in a withering phrase delivered emphatically to a climbing friend: "I think them . . . *simply* . . . ab*surd.*"

There is little evidence that Mallory was bisexual; late in life, Duncan Grant answered Everest historian Walt Unsworth's blunt inquiry about the matter, "No, certainly he was not." Yet James Strachey, Mallory's Cambridge classmate, testified in the affirmative. In any case, Mallory was so comfortable in the Cambridge-Bloomsbury milieu of platonized love and the cult of beauty that, years later, from the front in World War I, without a hint of embarrassment, he could write his wife, Ruth: "I had quite a thrill in the trenches yesterday on seeing a really beautiful face. . . . He had beautiful visionary eyes which looked at me thoughtfully before he answered my remarks."

During seasons in Wales and summers in the Alps, Mallory perfected his mountain craft. In his prime, his technique seems to have been as striking as his beauty, for colleague after colleague marveled at it. Ann Bridge remembered:

> He was never a showy climber; he did not go in for the minute precisions of style at all. On the contrary, he seemed to move on rocks with a sort of large, casual ease which was very deceptive when one came to try and follow him. When he was confronted with a pitch which taxed his powers, he would fling himself at it with a sort of angry energy, appearing to worry it as a terrier worries a rat, till he had mastered it.

Fear, added Bridge, was "something he had no experience of whatever."

Geoffrey Winthrop Young, the finest British climber of the generation before Mallory's, who would become the true mentor of his life, wrote, "He swung up rock with a long thigh, a lifted knee, and a ripple of irresistible movement." Robert Graves, later to become the great novelist, poet, and scholar, was taken climbing by Mallory as a schoolboy. In *Good-bye to All That*, Graves recalled that his tutor "used to go drunk with excitement at the end of his climbs." A fellow tutee testified, "He was quite the finest rock-climber I have ever seen, with a wonderful sense of balance."

On forays in the Alps, Mallory seemed completely at home on mountains that had severely intimidated many a British cragsman. Harry Tyndale captured Mallory's aplomb leading a steep ice pitch:

> He cut a superb staircase, with inimitable ease and grace and a perfect economy of effort. In watching George at work one was conscious not so much of physical strength as of suppleness and balance; so rhythmical and harmonious was his progress in any steep place, above all on slabs, that his movements appeared almost serpentine in their smoothness.

"Grace" and "balance"—those were the words repeated over and over by Mallory's companions to conjure up his alpine skills. "His movement in climbing was entirely his own," wrote Geoffrey Winthrop Young—himself well known for grace and balance.

> It contradicted all theory. He would set his foot high against any angle of smooth surface, fold his shoulder to his knee, and flow upward and upright again on an impetuous curve.... [T]he look, and indeed the result, were always the same—a continuous undulating movement so rapid and so powerful that one felt the rock either must yield, or disintegrate.

Mallory, Young added, "could make no movement that was not in itself beautiful. Inevitably he was a mountaineer, since climbing is the supreme opportunity for perfect motion."

Climbing with Young along the untrodden southeast ridge of the Nesthorn in the Alps in 1909, Mallory suffered the one serious fall of his alpine apprenticeship. Late in the afternoon, the men stood at the base of a vertical pillar, the last obstacle below the summit. Mallory took the lead and traversed out of sight around the corner. For his belay, Young simply stood on the ridge and laid the rope across a small "nick" in the corner of a slab. Unable to solve the pillar, Mallory appeared in sight, traversing back toward his partner, then, at the last minute, headed straight up toward an overhanging bulge, using his axe, as was the practice of the day, to hook small holds.

Young watched apprehensively, as he later wrote in *On High Hills*, as Mallory

> fought his way up magnificently, until all that remained below the rock cornice, which cut off everything else above from my sight, was his two boots. They were clinging, cat-like, and continued to cling for long seconds, to almost imperceptible irregularities on the walls of the rift. The mere sight of them made me breathless; and I tightened every muscle, ready to spring the rope on its nick.

Losing strength, Mallory launched a desperate "gymnastic backward swing" as he tried to top the overhang. "I saw the boots flash from the wall without even a scrape," remembered Young; "and, equally soundlessly, a grey streak flickered downward, and past me, and out of sight."

Mallory fell forty feet free, touching nothing, before the shock came on the rope. Young held on tight as the cord ground his hands into the slab. In the days before stretchy, strong nylon ropes, such falls usually caused the climbers' lifeline to break. Young anticipated as much. As he later put it,

> We were using that year a then rather popular Austrian woven rope, since entirely condemned. Whenever, in

later years, I have looked back at the tabulated rope-tests, which show that this rope is warranted to snap like a straw under the jerk of a man's weight falling from, I think, five feet, I have thought again of the transfigured second in which I realized that the rope had, miraculously, held.

Mallory was unhurt, and so unfazed by the fall that he hadn't even dropped his ice axe. Now he hooked his way up steep slabs back to his belayer. The two men continued up the Nesthorn, solving the pillar by another route, and Mallory led to the summit in the last light of the day. "He appeared, through the shadows," wrote Young, "to float like a thistledown up the last abrupt steps: up and up, through always denser cold and closer darkness."

Whether indeed, as Ann Bridge insisted, Mallory had no experience of fear, he related the attack on the previously unclimbed ridge of the Nesthorn in a letter to his mother as though it were merely another jolly outing in the Alps, rather than a desperate ascent that could well have proved fatal:

We were out twenty-one hours, and were altogether rather pleased with ourselves, as we started in bad weather which afterwards cleared up beautifully. The sunset from the Nesthorn was the most wonderful I have ever seen.

From such episodes, one might conclude that Mallory was a daredevil, supremely convinced of his own invulnerability, harboring perhaps a self-destructive demon. Yet David Pye, Mallory's climbing companion as well as his first biographer, insists that his friend was "very careful of unskilled performers, and very down on any clumsiness or carelessness." Reflecting on a climbing accident that befell a party tackling a route beyond their powers, he said—"in tones of angry grief"—"They had no *business* to be there!"

A month after the Nesthorn accident, Mallory suffered a more trivial fall that was to have far more important consequences. He was out walking with his sisters and friends near his parents' home in Birkenhead, when he came to a small sandstone cliff in a disused quarry. As biographer David Robertson puts it, "There was no need whatever to climb it, but George naturally made for it and started up."

Near the top of the short pitch he was soloing, Mallory ran into a troublesome sequence. One of the friends scrambled around to the top and lowered a rope, which George tried to grab just as he slipped, only to have it slide through his hands. With his feline agility, Mallory tried to spring outward and backward and land on his feet in the grass, but he came down hard with his right foot on a hidden stone.

Mallory assumed he had sprained the ankle, but for months it refused to heal. Writing Young in December, he reported, "Indeed it is still in a poor state and though I can walk well enough for a short distance, it is no good for the mountains." Mallory blamed only himself: "The whole affair is almost too disgusting to think of, the result chiefly of my obstinacy."

It was only eight years later, when the ankle caused him so much trouble on the Western Front during the Great War that he had to be invalided home, that Mallory learned he had broken the ankle in the 1909 fall; it had never properly healed. He underwent an operation that seemed to fix the problem, but seven years later, on his last expedition to Everest, he was still plagued by the injury. From Darjeeling in May 1924, full of optimism about the team's chances, he wrote Ruth: "The only doubts I have are whether the old ankle one way or another will cause me trouble."

After Cambridge, Mallory hoped to become a writer, and managed to publish a critical work called *Boswell the Biographer*, unread today. In his articles for the climbing journals, he went far beyond the dry recitations of passes gained and ridges traversed that were the norm of the day, striving for a lyrical flight to match the exaltation he felt in the mountains. In an ambitious 1914 essay he titled "The Mountaineer as Artist," Mallory spun out an elaborate conceit comparing a day in the Alps with a symphony. Here, as in the overearnest pages of many another young mountaineer-writer, a note of preciousness could creep in:

And so throughout the day successive moods induce the symphonic whole—allegro while you break the back of

an expedition and the issue is still in doubt; scherzo, perhaps, as you leap up the final rocks of the arête or cut
steps in a last short slope, with the ice-chips dancing and
swimming and bubbling and bounding with magic gai-
ety over the crisp surface in their mad glissade.

Yet as he matured, the loose lyricism of Mallory's prose ac-
quired a certain backbone, as he learned that he really had
something to say. He had a true gift for the aphoristic formula;
had he lived longer, Mallory might have become, as did Geoffrey Winthrop Young, one of the century's finest writers about
mountaineering. His most famous passage appears in an account of a difficult route on Mont Blanc, published in 1918 in
the *Alpine Journal:* "Have we vanquished an enemy? None but
ourselves. Have we gained success? That word means nothing
here."

There is perhaps a rueful irony in the fact that the single
phrase for which Mallory will forever be remembered was a
spontaneous retort, in the midst of a tiring American lecture
tour, to a journalist who asked him why he wanted to climb
Everest. "Because it is there," snapped Mallory, passing on to
posterity an apothegm as pithy as any Confucian riddle. Some
of Mallory's closest friends insisted that the response was
meant as an off-putting non sequitur, from a man weary in his
bones of being asked the same unanswerable question mountaineers have always been scolded with.

In the chapters he contributed to the official 1921 and 1922
Everest books, Mallory writes vividly and well; but so do most
of his teammates, so high were the standards of English education of the day. Noel Odell's and Teddy Norton's chapters in the
1924 book are the equal of Mallory's.

In 1910, at age twenty-four, to eke out a living, Mallory
took a teaching job at a public school called Charterhouse. He
poured himself into the job, on holiday taking students climbing in Wales and the Alps, just as R. L. G. Irving had taken him.
Some, such as Robert Graves, remained indebted to him the rest
of their days. But Mallory was too disorganized to be a really
effective teacher, too creative to be happy in his drudgerous and
sedentary post. As Graves put it, "George was wasted at Charterhouse."

Even so, he must have been a stimulating teacher. David Pye relates a stray remark that hints at the impishly subversive role Mallory played with his Charterhouse charges: "Imagine me to-morrow morning teaching the smallest boys about the fall of man! what the devil is one to say? It was such a wholly admirable business and God behaved so badly; mere petty jealousy!"

Politically, Mallory was a liberal on the far left, despite being a parson's son. He considered himself a Fabian, and championed such causes as women's suffrage and Irish home rule, traveling to the country in 1920 to witness for himself the barbarity of the English suppression. One night in Dublin, he was cross-examined in the glare of a flashlight by an official with a revolver in his hand, who apparently suspected him of being a rabid Sinn Feiner.

Starting in the spring of 1916, Mallory served on the French front during World War I, where he suffered his share of close calls—a whizzing bullet that passed between him and a nearby soldier, two friends blown apart by a shell as they ran a few paces behind him. At first, in letters home, he kept up the jaunty pretense that war was like some schoolboy sport: "Personally, I get some fun out of this sort of performance." "I played the game, on my way to the O.P., of shell-dodging for the first time. Quite an amusing game."

But the suffering and horror he saw on the front knocked much of that schoolboy preciousness out of George Mallory. There was no jauntiness left in the plain account of his discovery of the bodies of his two friends killed by the shell that exploded just behind him:

> I had not gone many paces when I saw that they were both lying face downwards. They seemed to be dead when we got to them. . . . They were very nice fellows— one of them quite particularly so. He had been with me up in the front line all day and proved the most agreeable of companions.

Mallory was lucky to be sent home, in May 1917, because of his bad ankle. Some of his closest friends were not so fortunate, such as his Cambridge classmate the poet Rupert Brooke, who died of blood poisoning; or Robert Graves, grievously wounded in the trenches; or Geoffrey Winthrop Young, who lost a leg above the knee, but would go on in his forties to climb at a high standard with an artificial limb.

In 1914, on a jaunt to Venice with friends, Mallory had met and fallen in love with Ruth Turner. She too was beautiful— "Botticellian" was his own word for her—and as he got to know her he formed a true union of souls with this quiet, loyal, well-educated woman. They were married only four months after meeting, just as Mallory had turned twenty-eight. He at once taught his bride to climb, hauling her along on far from trivial routes in Wales. Nor did he coddle or protect her. In the middle of a December gale on Snowdon, George, Ruth, and David Pye faced a "precipitously steep and terrifying" descent. When Ruth balked at plunging off the ridge, George took her by the shoulders and "simply pushed her forcibly over the edge! . . . Next he jumped over also and soon we were all gasping in comparative peace while the wind still roared overhead."

Despite her brave apprenticeship in climbing, despite an aesthetic compatibility between herself and her husband, Ruth's temperament was utterly different from George's. According to Pye, Ruth was "a person of the wisest simplicity and a transcendent practicalness." Her stability seemed to give Mallory an anchor in life. "A total stranger meeting both for the first time at some climbing centre, soon after their marriage," wrote Pye, "spoke of the shock of delight and astonishment which they produced. 'They seem too good to be true.' "

By the time he was fighting in the trenches in France, Mallory was the father of two infant girls—Clare, born in 1915, and Beridge, the year after. A third child, John, would be born in 1920. After being invalided home, Mallory had returned to the Western Front for the very last weeks of the war. When the Armistice came, he wrote Ruth, "What a wonderful life we will have together! What a lovely thing we *must* make of such a gift!"

So far as his biographers can ascertain, Ruth was the only important woman in Mallory's life. After a decade of marriage, their passion for each other seemed utterly undimmed, as their letters, collected in the archives of Magdalene College, testify.

In the summer of 1919, Mallory returned to the Alps for

the first time in seven years. Despite bad weather and companions far less bold or able than he, George pursued a joyous campaign of ascents. After an epic traverse of Mont Blanc in a storm, Mallory wrote Young a long letter, one phrase of which leaps out, in the retrospect of Everest 1924: "How incompetent tired men can become, going down!"

In the Alps, according to David Pye, Mallory demonstrated an uncanny eye for route-finding. "He was always drawn to the big and the unexplored—the great walls that mountaineers as a rule set aside as obviously impossible." When he failed on a climb, Mallory was devastated—" 'I was *heavy!'* he used to say in tones of deep disgust."

Mallory was happy to climb in Wales once more with Young, despite his mentor's artificial leg. To save his friend the agony of stumping along the approach trail, Mallory coaxed his little car up the Miner's Track to the very foot of Lliwedd.

But for Everest, Mallory might have settled down to a life of schoolteaching, dabbling as a writer, and climbing summers in the Alps. As early as 1919, however, rumors of a British reconnaissance of the approaches to the world's highest mountain were floating about. No Westerner had stood within forty miles of its flanks.

For a man of Mallory's restless spirit, this siren call could not go unheeded. He was by now unquestionably the finest mountaineer in Britain. But he was also a father and a schoolteacher, and he hesitated when the invitation came. It was Young who, in twenty minutes during a visit, persuaded Mallory (in David Robertson's words) "that Everest was an opportunity not to be missed: it would be an extraordinary adventure; and it would be something for George to be known by, in his future work as an educator or writer."

Thus, in a decision more pragmatic than spiritual, George Mallory walked open-eyed into the obsession that would make him famous, and that would cost him his life.

Dissonance

CA

AFTER A NIGHT of wretched "sleep," the five of us started down from Camp V on the morning of May 2. Above the North Col on the exposed snow ridge, I ran into Vladislav Terzeul, who goes by the name Slava, the strongest climber on a Ukrainian team that was preparing for its summit attempt. The first thing he said was, "Oh, you find Mallory?" I was taken aback, but I mumbled, "No, we haven't." Slava's question didn't mean the word was out. Everybody on the mountain knew what we had come for, so his was a natural question to ask.

At the North Col, I ran into Russell Brice. He's a strong New Zealander who had climbed Everest before, and was guiding clients up the north side. A great guy. He asked, "Well, did you find him?" Once more I muttered a denial.

The day before, as soon as I'd broadcast my coded messages about hobnails, Snickers and tea, and a mandatory group meeting, our teammates down at Advance Base and Base Camp knew that we were on to something. Simo had come on shortly afterward to warn us that our broadcasts were being monitored all over the mountain. Russell Brice had a very good radio setup, and he was one of the more meticulous monitors. Maybe he'd picked up something. But after Simo's warning, we'd shut down, maintaining virtual radio silence ever since.

We descended the icefall to ABC (Advance Base Camp) at 21,000 feet, to spend the night. There we met Simo and Thom Pollard, a videographer hired by *NOVA*. We came into camp hiking as a group so Thom could film our arrival. Dave Hahn and I always liked to joke about who walks in last, playing the humble role. Now the guys insisted that I walk in first. Simo had a huge grin on his face, and he was eager to hear the news, but we had to wait because there were all these folks from other expeditions milling around. Finally we hopped inside our dining tent, zipped it up, and that's when Dave told Eric what we had found.

He had expected that we'd reveal that we'd found Sandy Irvine. When we told him it was Mallory we'd discovered, all Simo could say was, "Wow, this is something else!"

We celebrated with cookies and tea, then decided to share the news with Russell Brice. I'd been feeling bad about telling him we hadn't found anything. Now Russell congratulated us warmly and agreed to keep the story under wraps.

That evening, Simo got on the satellite phone to call his girlfriend, Erin Copland, in Ashford, Washington, who was acting as expedition publicist. To his dismay, the first thing Erin said was, "The story's already out. *NOVA* broke the story yesterday in their dispatch."

At Base Camp, Liesl Clark, the producer of the *NOVA* film, had been sending reports almost daily to the PBS site on the Internet. MountainZone was also running dispatches. These were usually called in by satellite phone from the expedition members (mostly Simo) to a voice mailbox; the dispatches were then edited in Seattle and posted on the Internet. Dave Hahn put a lot of extra energy into his dispatches. This was Dave's second stint reporting for MountainZone on Everest. Instead of just calling in the first thing that came to mind, he'd stay up as late as 1:00 A.M. some nights typing well-crafted, very detailed reports onto a laptop, then sending them to Seattle.

So the expedition was being jointly covered on the Internet. When I got home, I read all the dispatches for the first time. Liesl's a good writer: her dispatches were lucid, comprehensive, and informative; she also transcribed interviews with us climbers. The MountainZone dispatches, on the other hand, tended to be fragmented and casual—which is understandable, given that the guys were usually calling Seattle at the end of a hard day. Just as understandably, they didn't take the broad view; even Dave's well-written reports tended to reflect whatever he'd been doing that day.

On May 1, the day of the search, Simo was tuned in at ABC, while Liesl listened at Base Camp. Jochen Hemmleb was right beside her, peering through his 200-power telescope, commenting over the radio on everything we did. During the early stages of the search, we were reporting our progress to Simo and Jochen. The conversation between Jochen and Jake about the oxygen bottle with blue paint on the end, identifying it as from the Chinese '75 expedition, was on the air. So was my discovery of the two modern bodies and the exchange between Andy Politz and me about where I was searching. It was only when I found Mallory and lapsed into the coded messages that we put up our guard.

Liesl wrote a clear play-by-play of monitoring our progress by radio and telescope from Base Camp. She reported my cryptic message, "Let's get together for Snickers and tea," and my call right after that for a "mandatory group meeting." Then she wrote, "This was the last we heard from the climbers for the day."

Liesl knew we'd made some kind of discovery. In her dispatch, she speculated out loud:

It became clear that what seemed like a normal series of radio calls was actually a signal that something was up. From his telescope, Hemmleb could see the five climbers coming together on the bottom edge of the snow terrace where Anker stood. Was "Snickers and tea" a code for something found? We are very aware of other expeditions listening in on our frequency, and had previously agreed that if the body were found we would keep the radio transmissions to a minimum. This "mandatory group meeting" which sent [Andy] Politz some 330 feet down from his search position could only mean that Anker had found something. But what?

At the end of that day, when we'd reached Camp V, we got on the radio, just to let Simo know that everybody was safe and sound. We kept mum about Mallory, but Dave couldn't resist sneaking in, "Jochen, you are going to be a happy man."

Liesl closed her dispatch with that provocative teaser. She sent it off, and PBS/*NOVA* must have gotten it up on the Internet late on May 1, U.S. time. The dispatch proved indeed to be a bombshell. Meanwhile, between April 29 and May 2, the MountainZone site had no dispatches at all. Dave, of course, was busy with the search, and once Simo learned about our discovery, he wanted to decide how best to break the news to the world.

When Simo found out from Erin that *NOVA* had scooped MountainZone, he was furious. It wasn't simply that he was the chief reporter for MountainZone; Simo had entered into an exclusive agreement with the company and felt betrayed. The only private way to communicate with Liesl, across the thirteen miles from ABC to Base Camp, was by e-mail. So on May 2, Simo sent her a really frosty e-mail message. After reprimanding her for "cybercasting (as opposed to running an educational Web site, as you professed)," he made this threat: "I am forced to take action in this matter and have no choice but to ask that you either cease cybercasting, or that you will have to leave the expedition."

Liesl was really shaken up. When I got down to Base Camp, she confided in me, "What did I do to deserve this?" Later, Simo complained that MountainZone and *NOVA* had an explicit agreement that *NOVA* would observe a twenty-four-hour moratorium on all news, to give MountainZone the first crack at anything spectacular. But Peter Potterfield and Simonson both subsequently clarified that the twenty-four-hour moratorium came out of this blowup: before May 2, there was no such agreement. In sum, Liesl simply did what any good reporter would do with breakthrough news.

I first met Simo on Denali (Mount McKinley) in 1989, when we were on the mountain on separate expeditions. He was guiding clients, while I was collecting granite rocks for a geological profile of the mountain. Simo's big, tall, forty-four years old, with dark hair and eyes, a strong mountaineer who's become a full-time guide. He learned his trade on Rainier under Lou Whittaker, whose RMI (Rainier Mountaineering, Incorporated) was for years the only guide service on the mountain. A few years ago, Eric broke away to form IMG (International Mountain Guides), of which he's now co-owner. IMG is ambitious; they guide Kilimanjaro and Vinson, the highest peak in Antarctica, as well as Cho Oyu, Shisha Pangma, and Everest in the Himalaya. The other guys on our climbing team had worked with Eric either at IMG or RMI.

Simo climbed Everest in 1991 via the north side, on his third expedition to the mountain. He's paid his dues in the high-stakes game of high-altitude climbing. This year he was not as driven to go high as the other guys. Instead he used his energy to manage the expedition.

Simo's absolutely brilliant at logistics. I couldn't believe how well everything ran on this expedition. Eric's care for the Sherpas is exemplary. He makes sure the Sherpas are treated as equals, puts the highest priority on their safety, and pays the best wages. As a result, his Sherpas are intensely loyal to him. On the mountain he's extremely thorough, knows the best camp sites, knows the value of having new fixed ropes in place. He's got expeditionary climbing down to a science.

Eric is pretty autocratic: he operates best when he's in control. If you make a mistake, he lets you know it in no uncertain terms. He'll let you know what he expects of you, whether you are a Sherpa or a team member or even a trekker. Like most Everest expeditions, we brought along trekkers who paid good money to join us at Base Camp, then culminate their journey with a climb to ABC. The day after they arrived, two trekkers simply took off without telling anybody where they were going. Tap, Jake, and I marched up a frozen ravine looking for the fellows at dusk. A night in the open would not only have threatened their lives, it could have seriously impeded our own climbing plans. The two trekkers made it back to camp an hour after dark. Simo ordered them off the expedition, sending them home the next day, no money refunded. Perhaps he overreacted, but I think the move was justified, that it gave out a clear message about leadership and responsibility.

Talk in the dining tent invariably drifted to politics. Simo's well to the right of most of us, and he liked to tweak our liberal sensibilities. When Jake Norton would start talking about Tibetan independence, which he cares passionately about, Simo would say, "No, Jake, it's not 'save Tibet,' it's 'pave Tibet.' "

The blowup about NOVA scooping MountainZone brings up another interesting point. More and more in the future, expeditions to remote places on earth are going to be covered live, in "real time," over the Internet. And even the proponents of this kind of you-are-there reportorial immediacy have only begun to think out the aesthetics and ethics of that kind of journalism.

My collaborator, David Roberts, told me about his own experience a couple of years back in Ethiopia, where he made the first descent of a major river with a bunch of rafting guides from Sobek. He was writing dispatches every night for the Microsoft online adventure magazine, *Mungo Park*.

Early in the expedition, the team doctor got terribly sick. He lay there puking and moaning, and his temperature went over 105° F. It was truly a life-or-death predicament. The expedition ground to a halt while its leaders debated whether to try to arrange a helicopter rescue, which would have been a perilous operation. This was Roberts's dilemma: should he report in real time what was happening to the doctor? Was that the proper way for his wife to learn what was going on? Nothing else was happening on the river, and the team was in the middle of a genuinely dramatic crisis. But Roberts had to ponder the possibility that if he sent out the news, he might launch a rescue effort even without the team leaders calling for one. In the end, he chose to write the truth. Fortunately, the doctor's fever broke and he was able to finish the expedition.

On May 1, what was Liesl supposed to do, except report what she saw and heard on what had turned out to be the most dramatic day so far, on this expedition that hundreds of thousands of Web users were following online?

In any event, once Simo learned from Erin that *NOVA* had already put out some kind of hot news on the Internet, he and Dave stayed up late into the night writing their own dispatch. It went up on the morning of May 3, and it was the definitive story. Eric wrote, "I have some huge news to announce, so I hope everyone is sitting down and ready for this one. . . . I'm pleased to announce that the 1999 Mallory & Irvine Research Expedition has found the remains of George Mallory, lost on Mount Everest on June 8th, 1924." Dave went on to describe the discovery, and to offer a rationale for partially excavating the body: "We didn't want to disturb him, he'd been lying there for 75 years, but at the same time we thought what better tribute to the man than to try and find out if he had summitted Mt. Everest in 1924."

For the first time, MountainZone ran a special caveat at the head of the dispatch: "This copyrighted content is exclusive to MountainZone.com and may not be used on any other website or news media."

As if to make up for being scooped, MountainZone now flooded the Web with news. By May 4, they had posted phoned-in dispatches not only from Dave and Eric, but from Jake, Tap, Andy, and me, each giving our side of the discovery story. At the site, Dave had shot a lot of pictures with a digital camera. Now at ABC he downloaded and digitally transmitted the images via satellite phone to Seattle. Eventually, MountainZone had on its site a dramatic photo of Mallory's body from the waist up, his bare, alabaster back looming in the center, the powerful muscles flexed, his fingers planted in the scree. At the time, we just thought of the photo as an important aid in documenting our find. We had no idea how controversial that picture would prove to be.

On the morning of May 3, at ABC, an Italian-American climber, Fabrizio Zangrilli, walked over to our camp and said, "Hey, you guys found Mallory. I just heard it on the BBC." That was our first inkling just how big the news was playing around the world. We went into Fabrizio's radio tent and got the BBC on the shortwave. The story came up on the hour. There was Erin's voice, talking about the discovery, and suddenly Sir Edmund Hillary with a short comment. It was amazing how fast the media had moved.

At noon we started down to Base Camp, at 17,200 feet. We got there about dusk. Everyone was ecstatic, giving us big hugs. Jochen came over and served me tea and some little Snickers bars, while the camera rolled. That evening we celebrated with a liberal dram of Scotch for all.

The same evening, we filmed our initial scrutiny of the artifacts. The mood in the tent was pensive, as each of us weighed the scope of the discovery. The next day, we were concerned about moisture damaging the objects, so I built a drying table to spread them on. Then Jochen took over the process, as planned, inventorying, measuring, and describing each object. He was very fussy about the procedure that had to be followed. First he had to hear our account of the find, then he examined and catalogued each artifact, then he reviewed the video. Like a connoisseur savoring a wine, Jochen relished every detail.

Jochen, Liesl, and I opened the letters that Mallory had wrapped in his handkerchief and read them carefully. The next day, Liesl made a transcription on her laptop, as backup in case anything happened to the originals.

Meanwhile, we learned from Erin in Seattle that there was a huge demand for photos of Mallory's body. For expedition climbers, used to going off to remote places where we'd be out of touch with the rest of the world for months at a time, it was hard to realize what the wonders of modern technology might mean. But it began to dawn on us that while we were still on the mountain, with the trip far from over, pictures we had taken could be digitally transmitted to the U.S., sold, and published. We realized there might be a hefty chunk of cash coming in for the photo rights.

We had a group meeting at Base Camp to discuss how to handle photo rights. Prior to the expedition, the climbing team had agreed to pool the proceeds and divide them equally. Liesl suggested we turn the digital images over to Gamma Liaison, a well-respected agency she had worked with in the past. That seemed like a good idea.

It quickly became clear that a bidding war for exclusive photo rights had already begun among the magazines and newspapers on at least three continents. For young guys like Tap and Jake, struggling to make ends meet as climbing guides, you could understand the temptation to sell to the highest bidder. From one photo, they might make as much money as they could in three weeks of guiding on Denali. Dave wanted to sell the pictures to as many publications as would run them, to give himself the maximum exposure as photographer, a profession he's serious about.

I felt we should aim for the publication with the highest credibility, in hopes that it would put the most positive spin on mountaineering. Climbers get maligned all too often. Every time some drunk falls off a road cut, the media call it a climbing accident. Or people see *Cliffhanger*, and they think that's what climbing's all about. I make my living at climbing, and I'm very sensitive about how our sport is portrayed. I didn't want our expedition to be seen as a bunch of thrill seekers or treasure hunters.

For the same reason, when the guys talked about what they'd do with the money, I said that I planned to give mine to some charity that would help out the people of Tibet. I was always mindful of how fortunate I was to be here climbing on this great mountain, which we couldn't have done, for instance, without the help of our Tibetan yak herders. I'm comfortable with the living I make climbing. I saw the find as a way to generate goodness.

In the end, the photo went to the highest bidder. *Newsweek* won the auction in the U.S.; for a while, we were hearing numbers upward of $14,000, though in the end they may have paid a lot less. Unfortunately, in the U.K. and Australia tabloid newspapers won out.

For about a week, however, we were flying high—everybody seemed happy about our discovery, everyone showered us with congratulations. Then we began to hear the first notes of discord. They came principally out of Britain, and we were shocked when we learned that what we had done at 26,700 feet had elicited not only praise, but savage criticism.

THE NEWS ABOUT MALLORY indeed galvanized the world. *Newsweek* ran a responsible story with its exclusive photo of the mummified body, but refused at first to pay for the picture, because *Time* had "bootlegged" the same image, running a picture of the cover of the Australian paper that had broken the story, complete with "exclusive" photo. Unfortunately, the British and Australian tabloids covered the discovery with all the sensitivity of a two-headed baby tale or Princess Di séance.

At first, even among seasoned mountaineers, there was great excitement about the possibility that the find lent credence to the notion that Mallory and Irvine had reached the summit. Andy Politz's insight—that Mallory's having put his

goggles in his pocket meant that the accident had come at dusk
or after—got all too easily translated into a scenario in which
the pair fell as they descended after reaching the top.

Thus the German magazine *Stern*, running its own exclusive, titled its cover story, above a portrait of Mallory inset
against a Himalayan ice scape, "War er der Erste?"—"Was he
the first?" *Stern* also was at pains to portray its own country's
fair-haired boy, Jochen Hemmleb, as the genius behind the discovery: a call-out from the article read, "Directed by the German over the radio, the search-troop found the dead body."

By May 3, only two days after the find, *NOVA* had an in-
terview with David Breashears up on its Web site. The director
and cinematographer of the groundbreaking Everest IMAX
film, as well as of a 1987 documentary called *Everest: The Mystery of Mallory and Irvine*, Breashears had been to the mountain on fourteen expeditions, summitting four times. He said, "I
think it's incredibly exciting that they've finally found George
Mallory's body." Breashears went on to speculate that it was
not surprising the camera wasn't found with Mallory, for it
would have made more sense that Irvine would be in charge of
taking pictures of the leader—"the man of Everest . . . George
Mallory." Breashears held out hope that a subsequent search
would come up not only with Irvine's body, but with the camera
that could solve the mystery for good. He closed with a tribute
in the same vein as Conrad Anker's awe-struck *pensée* as he had
sat beside Mallory's body: "All those years that I've been going
to Everest . . . thinking about these incredible men trying for
the summit of Everest in 1924, in cotton wind suits and tweed
jackets, for me, I feel a bit reassured and a bit resolved that we
know where George Mallory is."

Breashears later vividly took issue with the Hemmleb-as-
director spin on the story: "All Hemmleb did was feed some
data into the computer and think he'd reinvented information.
Mallory wasn't a dot on the ocean floor, and those guys weren't
submersibles. Conrad Anker was the only real climber on the
team. The reason they found Mallory is because Conrad used
his climber's eye to figure out where to look."

At first, especially in England, the discovery was hailed as a
splendid event, renewing the nation's sense of pride in its Everest pioneers. "Admiration grows with hindsight," editorialized

the *Times* of London. "Mallory was in a long tradition of English adventurers and sportsmen whose nonchalance and gentlemanly demeanor masked fierce ambition."

"There remains something wonderful about the spirit of play," echoed the *Guardian*, "that carries people into contests where there is no material reward, no point but the thing itself."

With the publication of the photos—the one showing Mallory's bare back, his fingers clawing at the scree, his face frozen into the ground, the other zooming in on the man's vulnerable, naked left leg cradling the hopelessly fractured right one—another note emerged in the public response. Some viewers found an eerie fascination in the images, like Boris Johnson of the *Daily Telegraph*, who wrote, "Something about these pictures causes the nape to prickle. Not that they are gruesome: no, there is something about that bleached torso which is already sculptural, at one remove."

Yet other commentators, including some of the most famous climbers in the world, were outraged by the publication of the photos. "I'm absolutely appalled by this. Words can't express how disgusted I am. . . . These people don't deserve to be called climbers," Sir Chris Bonington told the London *Observer*. Bonington had led the landmark 1975 first ascent of the southwest face of Everest, then, ten years later, had become at fifty the oldest man to summit (though his record stood for only nine days). Sir Edmund Hillary, whose first response had been positive, changed his mind, deploring the notion that "the expedition members should flog off the photograph of this heroic figure."

Mallory's grandson George Mallory II, who had climbed Everest by the north ridge in 1995, weighed in: "Frankly, it makes me bloody angry. . . . It's like digging for diamonds, without having to do any of the digging."

Even Audrey Salkeld, who had spent years becoming the leading expert on Mallory, and who was serving as a consultant on the *NOVA* film, was disturbed: "I'm horrified it's got to this stage," she told the *Observer*. "I feel very uncomfortable about it."

Eric Simonson had maintained that all the expedition's actions at the site, down to the taking of the DNA sample, had

ABOVE: George Mallory

LEFT: Andrew "Sandy" Irvine

BELOW: Mallory (right) and Siegfried Herford resting between climbs at Pen-y-Pass, Wales, 1913.

4

5

ABOVE LEFT: George Finch wearing the cumbersome oxygen equipment in 1922. The whole rig weighed more than thirty pounds.

ABOVE RIGHT: Mallory (left) and Norton approaching their 1922 high point of 26,000 feet, setting a short-lived world altitude record.

BELOW: Most of the 1924 expedition at Base Camp. Standing, left to right: Irvine, Mallory, Norton, Odell, MacDonald (trading agent). Sitting, left to right: Shebbeare (assistant transport officer), Geoffrey Bruce, Somervell, Beetham. Among the climbers, Noel and Hazard are missing from the picture.

6

Irvine tinkering with the oxygen apparatus on Everest.

Somervell's dramatic photo of Norton pushing toward the high point on June 4. The summit pyramid rises in the background.

9

The last known photo of Mallory (left) and Irvine, setting off from the North Col on June 6.

The 1999 Mallory & Irvine Research Expedition. Standing, left to right: Dave Hahn, Thom Pollard, Conrad Anker, Tap Richards, Eric Simonson. Kneeling, left to right: Lee Meyers (doctor), Andy Politz, Jake Norton.

The classic view of the north face of Everest from the terminus of the Rongbuk Glacier (Base Camp).

10

11

12

Puja at Base Camp performed by monks from the Rongbuk Monastery, April 1. Andy Politz is at center. Everest is barely visible through the smoke in the background.

13

Rongbuk Monastery.

Conrad Anker at the base of the ice chimney en route to the North Col.

14

15

Looking down from the north ridge of Everest toward Changtse (24,831 feet). In the foreground are tents from Camp V.

RIGHT: Conrad Anker resting en route to Camp VI, with oxygen mask in place.

BELOW: Climbing to Camp VI, May 16. Left to right: Dave Hahn, Tap Richards, Andy Politz.

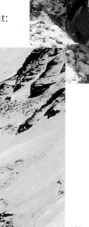

16

17

18   Around noon May 1, Conrad Anker with the body of George L. Mallory.

LEFT: Detail of Mallory's boot showing the v-shaped hobnails. On loose, shaley rock these boots excelled, but on hardened snow and ice, the climber would have to chop steps for a secure purchase.

BELOW: Artifacts found on Mallory: folding knife, small scissors, phosphorus matches, pencil, zinc oxide and beef lozenges (on the scarf), safety pin, altimeter, fastening strap (possibly from the oxygen apparatus), goggles, various bits of twine.

19

20

21

Conrad Anker snapped this photo of Dave Hahn as the two climbers
approached the summit of Everest on May 17.

been approved beforehand by someone in the Mallory family. In Santa Rosa, California, however, Clare Millikan, at eighty-three the eldest of Mallory's three children, was upset that nobody from the expedition had contacted her before the discovery.

Had the team set forth last spring on a traditional expedition, all this public response would have emerged only after they had returned to the U.S. to report their great find. But now, thanks to the satellite phone and the Internet, even as they rested at Base Camp, with other important goals still to pursue, the party was plunged into the midst of the controversy. Here lay another peculiar twist to what might be called postmodern exploration: the reaction of a worldwide audience to an adventure still in the process of unfolding could determine crucial turns in the course of that adventure.

Another by-product of this postmodern expedition's self-narration in "real time" was a certain aesthetic loss, compared to the chronicles of earlier exploits on Everest. After each of the 1921, 1922, and 1924 expeditions, the members labored for months to compile monumental volumes recounting their journeys. Those books—*Mount Everest: The Reconnaissance, 1921;* *The Assault on Mount Everest, 1922;* and *The Fight for Everest*—have become classics. Chapters by Mallory, Noel Odell, and Teddy Norton contain some of the canonic passages in the rich literature of mountaineering.

By contrast, in the flurry of MountainZone dispatches in which the teammates struggled to express their feelings on May 1, 1999, they managed to produce only inarticulate outbursts of enthusiasm. "We just came down from the search area," reported Jake Norton, "and it was a pretty interesting time." "I'm still blown away by yesterday," offered Dave Hahn: "we found George Mallory and it was an incredible day." "It was really neat to be there with George Mallory," gushed Tap Richards. The usually thoughtful Conrad Anker came up with the lame aperçu, "He had been there quite a while, and there was something very, very subtle about his being there, not really scary and violent." (Compare Odell's musing on Mallory going all-out for the summit, in *The Fight for Everest:* "And who of us that has wrestled with some Alpine giant in the teeth of a gale, or in a race with the darkness, could hold back when such a victory, such a triumph of human endeavour, was within our grasp?")

No doubt the 1999 team's blatherings were merely the detritus of the age of the sound bite. But the lack of opportunity to reflect on a powerful experience, along with the fact that, thanks to the Internet, everything the team did and blurted out was at once available for public consumption, helped power the emotional roller coaster the expedition now rode.

It had simply never occurred to Simonson and his partners that photographing and filming the corpse, or rifling through its pockets, might provoke disapproval. Now the angry and critical reaction from mountaineering heroes such as Bonington and Hillary deeply dismayed the team. Eric Simonson called a group meeting to discuss what Anker had dubbed the "dissonance." One upshot of that conference surfaced when Simonson announced, in a post-expedition press conference, that all profits from the sale of Mallory photos would go not into the pockets of team members, but to "Himalayan charities to be determined later."

The members were only beginning to recognize the fact that extremely knotty legal tangles might well hang over the "artifacts" and the letters, which they hoped to carry back to the States. To whom did the stuff ultimately belong? Was it a case of finders keepers; were the team members, in Anker's pithy phrase, "the Mel Fishers of high-altitude climbing," treating Mallory like a long-lost Spanish galleon? Or did Mallory's estate have a prior claim? Someone in England had come forth to argue that the gear found with Mallory belonged to the companies that had originally sponsored the 1924 expedition. As for the letters and notes and the right to publish their contents, which copyright laws applied? The Chinese or Tibetan regulations of today, or Britain's in 1924?

Through the Internet, the team learned about the debacle of the accidental bombing of the Chinese embassy in Belgrade by NATO planes, and about the rabid anti-American protests that act had provoked in China. The fear grew among the members that, as they made their way out of Tibet, Chinese authorities might confiscate the artifacts. For that reason, Simonson did not at first tell the team's Han Chinese liaison officer about finding Mallory. (The man learned of the discovery only by listening to Chinese radio.) And when trekker Shellene Scott left Base Camp to go home to the States on May 9, she carried some of the objects in her baggage.

As Anker had laid out the artifacts to dry at Base Camp, and Hemmleb had pored over them, making notes, it became increasingly clear that even such humble belongings as a box of matches and a tin of beef lozenges had both forensic and symbolic value. For many years now, Robert Falcon Scott's diary, found by his teammates beside his dead body eight months after his demise on the return journey from the South Pole, has lain under glass in the reading room of the British Museum, turned open to its famous last page. Surely Mallory's bent goggles, his monogrammed handkerchief, had a comparable numen.

Higher on the mountain, Dave Hahn had cursorily glanced through the letters the team had found wrapped in the handkerchief. One was from Mallory's sister Mary, another from his brother, Trafford; both were full of family news and holiday chat. A third, though also newsy, had a line indicating a deeper intimacy. Trying to make out the signature, Hahn concluded that it read "Sweetie," and jumped to the obvious conclusion. As he wrote in his May 4 MountainZone dispatch: "There were some remarkable things that turned up . . . culminating in a perfectly preserved letter from his wife, worn on his chest, close to his heart."

Now, down at Base Camp, Anker, Hemmleb, and Liesl Clark read the letters more carefully, as Clark transcribed their contents onto her laptop. Studying the signature on the third letter, they realized that it read not "Sweetie" (by all odds an unlikely sobriquet for Ruth to have assumed), but "Stella." Suddenly the unexplained third letter seemed a potential bombshell. The epistle had been posted from London S.W. 4, but had no return address; it had been written on the stationery of a posh English men's club, with the letterhead scratched out.

Who was Stella? Was this a love letter? Reading and rereading the sentences, Clark and Anker could not decide. The intimate phrase might just have sprung from the effusive vocabulary current among friends and relatives in the 1920s in Britain; yet what about the apparent efforts to conceal the writer's identity and the letter's provenience?

The Stella letter became a closely guarded secret within the expedition. Clark could imagine what the English tabloids would do with this revelation ("Lost Mountaineer's Secret Lover")—with little more than the knowledge that such a letter existed and had been carried next to Mallory's heart on his summit attempt. Yet, as so often happens with a confidence shared among too many independent souls, rumors about the Stella letter leaked out.

Eric Simonson tried hard to control the gossip. On May 7, in a MountainZone dispatch, he corrected Hahn's error, in as vague a fashion as he could manage:

> For the record, there were several different letters from various family members. The handwriting on some of them is a little tough to read, and it's not entirely clear whether the letter from his wife was in fact from his wife, but we're working on that.

There is no doubt that, as late as 1924, Mallory was still deeply in love with his wife. His long letters to her from the expedition breathe that passion, and the pain of separation: "How I wish I had you with me! With so much leisure we should have enjoyed the time together. . . . Great love to you, dearest one."

Yet at the same time, those letters adumbrate certain recent problems the couple had faced: "I know I have rather often been cross and not nice, and I'm very sorry." "We went through a difficult time together in the autumn." Mallory's biographers have always assumed that the troubles thus alluded to had to do with career and money, and with the many months Mallory was away on Everest.

Upon his return to the U.S., Simonson kept the letters under lock and key at the Washington State Historical Museum. In late July, he traveled to California to present the letters to Clare Millikan and her brother, John Mallory, who traveled to the U.S. from South Africa to retrieve them. Her memory prodded by the Stella letter, Clare remembered one Stella Mellersh, a woman who had married a cousin of Ruth Mallory's. She had been a generation older than George Mallory.

Rick Millikan, Clare's son and Mallory's grandson, carefully read the letter and decided that the apparently intimate phrase had been misread at Base Camp: all it really said, Millikan thought, was something like, "Much love to you, George." Simonson pointed out some penciled scribblings on the envelope in Mallory's hand, which he thought might be an inventory of oxygen bottles. It occurred to Simonson and Millikan that perhaps Mallory had carried the Stella letter so high mainly to use the envelope as a piece of note paper!

From this California meeting, John Mallory carried the letters back to Magdalene College, Cambridge, where they were to be archived with the existing Mallory correspondence. Eventually scholars will be able to puzzle over the Stella letter to their hearts' content, determining whether it really is an intimate message from a phantom lover or only a pleasant note from a distant older relative.

As striking in its own way as the anomalous Stella letter was the absence of any missive from Ruth in that neatly folded handkerchief. On the journey from Darjeeling, and even at Base Camp, Mallory had received letters from his wife. Clare Millikan was told at age eight that her father carried a photo of Ruth, which he intended to leave on the summit. Among those who most wanted to believe Mallory could have made it to the top, here was another circumstantial argument: perhaps the great mountaineer had indeed left the most precious thing he could carry—a letter from or a photo of his wife—among the summit snows.

ON MAY 8, WE DESCENDED from Base Camp to the Rongbuk Monastery—the highest monastery in the world, destroyed by the Chinese during the Cultural Revolution, but mostly rebuilt since. Liesl shot some film footage there, but the main idea was to bide our time, to fatten up and recharge prior to heading back up for the second and more demanding summit phase of the expedition.

My method of recharging is to eat all the junk food I can, all day long. Candy bars, potato chips, little bits of cheese, sardines—anything with a high fat content. The downside of this day-long grazing was that when we were served dinner, I didn't have much appetite for a plateful of rice with stewed cabbage, because I'd been eating a lot of chocolate. But calories are calories. It's not so much a question of fattening up as of trying to keep weight on. I knew I had already lost weight on the expedition. My legs were getting thinner.

At Bouddanath, in Kathmandu, at the beginning of the expedition, we had had a *puja* ceremony, a blessing for the expedition. Later, on April 1, the monks from the Rongbuk Monastery came up to Base Camp to give us a second *puja*. The high lama who led the ceremony at Bouddanath had tied a red prayer knot around my neck. Three months later, I haven't taken it off: it's a common Buddhist practice to leave it on until it disintegrates.

At the *puja* at Base Camp, we had trucked in some juniper to burn, and we made offerings to the monks. I gave them a bunch of Skittles—a hard candy I sometimes eat when I'm rock-climbing—some turkey jerky, and a Coca-Cola. The monks tossed rice around, which all the birds came to feed on, and they smeared tsampa flour on our faces and gave us tsampa cake to eat.

Some of the guys on our expedition didn't take the *puja* very seriously. Peter Firstbrook, the BBC director, was washing his socks at the Rongbuk *puja*. You wouldn't wash your socks during services at St. Paul's Cathedral. Other Westerners just more or less tolerated the ceremony. You can see that in the way Dave Hahn wrote up the Base Camp *puja* on Mountain-Zone:

> We had our Puja yesterday. That is when we put the packing and planning on hold and get down to some serious begging. The Puja is a ceremony designed to get some good credit with the gods, seeing as how we are now going to get up to our eyeballs in this thing. Really, it is for the Sherpas and their brand of mountain Buddhism. We try to show our respect for them and their beliefs by allowing the ceremony.

The *puja* is indeed a deeply serious ceremony for the Sherpas. And I take it very seriously too. At the Bouddanath *puja*, from a little tray of offerings the lamas passed around, I picked out a walnut that I intended to leave on the summit.

I wouldn't call myself a Buddhist, but I have a great admiration for the religion. The Dalai Lama says his religion is kindness. If you're going to be kind to yourself, be kind to your friends, to your partner, your family, the animals, the trees. I believe in that. I also believe in karma. It's not just a matter of the right actions; you have to have the right intentions as well.

There was the same kind of range in response to the *puja* way back in the 1920s. Expedition member Bentley Beetham, in *The Fight for Everest*, the official book from 1924, describes coming upon a service in progress in the Rongbuk Monastery as the team left the mountain. "Hitherto we had felt nothing but revulsion for the lamas," Beetham writes; after all, these Buddhist monks were idolaters, worshiping false gods. Yet as he watched, he got caught up in the ceremony, until he had to admit that it was "the most impressive, the most moving service I, for one, have ever attended." Beetham was so moved that his cultural superiority was tempered: "These Tibetans may be wrong, they may be deceived, but they are obviously in earnest; an English congregation may not be deceived, but are they in earnest?"

As the international fuss about our discovery started to calm down a bit, we planned the second stage of our expedition. We'd hoped to make a second search for Sandy Irvine and the camera. But it had snowed a fair amount since May 1, and we weren't so sanguine about our chances of making a second find.

And four of us—Dave Hahn, Tap Richards, Jake Norton, and I—wanted to have a shot at the summit. In addition, I had a personal aspiration, which Simo and I had discussed even before we left the States. I wanted to try to free-climb the Second Step. That, for me, was the crucial test of the likelihood that Mallory and Irvine could have made the summit.

To free-climb a pitch is to scale it using only one's hands and feet, without relying on artificial objects—pitons, machined nuts, even ladders—to gain upward progress.

Some background is in order. On June 4, 1924, Teddy Norton had reached a height calculated as 28,126 feet by traversing west across the north face and entering the Great Couloir. In 1933, Frank Smythe exactly matched that high point, which stood, in the absence of any sure knowledge of Mallory and Irvine's achievement, as the world altitude record until 1952, when the Swiss Raymond Lambert and the Sherpa Tenzing Norgay turned back on the South Col route only 800 feet below the summit.

The Great Couloir would prove a feasible route up the north side of Everest, as Reinhold Messner demonstrated in making his amazing oxygenless solo ascent in 1980. But we know this was not the route followed by Mallory and Irvine, because Odell saw them high on the skyline of the north ridge.

The Second Step is a ninety-foot-high, nearly vertical cliff that interrupts the north ridge at 28,230 feet. There's no way of skirting it: you have to tackle it head-on. Unless Mallory and Irvine climbed it, the first men to grapple with this formidable obstacle were the Chinese team in 1960. By their own account, which appeared in a propaganda organ called *China Reconstructs*, after an all-out effort in which one climber took off his boots and gloves and tried the cliff in stocking feet, a partner solved the climb by standing on another teammate's shoulders. Three men then went on to the top in the dark.

Or so the article claims. I've always had my doubts about that purported ascent, and so have others.

The first well-documented ascent of the north ridge, also by Chinese, came in 1975, during the expedition on which Wang Hongbao found his "old English dead." Aware of the difficulty of the Second Step, the team hauled a ladder up to the crux and tied it to pitons they pounded in place. All subsequent ascents of the north ridge have used the ladder and/or the myriad fixed ropes now in place on the Step.

Mallory and Irvine, of course, had had no ladder. So if I could free-climb the Second Step and judge its difficulty, that would tell us a lot about whether Mallory and Irvine could have pulled it off in 1924, in hobnailed boots and tweed jackets, holding a thin cotton rope in an anchorless gentleman's belay.

We were just getting organized to head back up the mountain when something happened that put all our plans on hold. That spring, among the several expeditions on the north side of

Everest, we'd been the first to get up high, to fix ropes and pitch Camps IV and V. Following right after us was the strong Ukrainian team, who, despite the language barrier, had become our friends.

They'd decided early on that May 8 was to be their summit day. Unfortunately, May 8 turned out to be the worst day of our forty so far on the mountain. Even down at the Rongbuk Monastery, it was snowing on us. I could see that the weather wasn't just the usual afternoon buildup of clouds. There were squalls and flurries developing into a major storm.

We decided to head back up to Base Camp. The weather got worse and worse. By 9:00 P.M., we knew the Ukrainians were in serious trouble. Instead of climbing the mountain ourselves, we were going to have to go out and try to rescue them.

Mallory of Everest

DR

THE 1921 RECONNAISSANCE OF EVEREST, pursued through the monsoon summer and into the autumn season, was in many respects a colossal mess. The party's talents were wildly uneven, with several over-the-hill, out-of-shape veterans in leadership positions. Entrusted with choosing a team, the Everest Committee—a national board of exploratory experts formed for the express purpose of claiming the "Third Pole" for the Empire—valued years of hill-walking and Himalayan rambling over technical mountaineering skills.

From the start, Mallory was at serious odds with the team's leader, Charles Howard-Bury, and its climbing leader, Harold Raeburn, both much older than he. Of the former, he wrote Ruth, "He is not a tolerant person. He is well-informed and opinionated and doesn't at all like anyone else to know things he doesn't know. For the sake of peace, I am being very careful not to broach certain subjects of conversation." Of Raeburn: "He is dreadfully dictatorial about matters of fact, and often wrong."

Before the party even got near Mount Everest, the well-liked but fifty-year-old Scottish doctor, A. M. Kellas, died of dysentery. His teammates buried him on a stony hillside, in what Mallory called "an extraordinarily affecting little ceremony."

In view of the 1999 controversy over scoops on the Internet and secrets guarded by Simonson's teammates, it is interesting to note that the same kinds of worries afflicted the first expedition to approach the world's highest mountain. The Everest Committee had made a deal with the *Times* of London for exclusive coverage, irritating rivals such as the *Daily Telegraph.* Even before the team had found Everest, one of the committee's potentates wrote the surveyor-general of India, expressing his fears about "unexpected leakage," and fingering a reporter for the Calcutta *Morning Post* as a particularly dangerous suspect. A kindred paranoia had dictated an oath that all the team members had been required to sign before leaving England, enjoining them "not to hold any communication with the press or with any press agency or publisher, or to deliver any public lecture" without the approval of the Everest Committee.

So a motley assortment of mountaineers and travelers, already torn by jealousies and disparate ambitions, stumbled toward Everest in the wrong season. George Bernard Shaw later memorably characterized a group portrait of the team as looking "like a picnic in Connemara surprised by a snowstorm."

By mid-June, with the party still far from the mountain, with Kellas dead and Raeburn laid low by diarrhea and injuries incurred in twice falling off his horse, the number of able mountaineers left on the expedition had dwindled to two: Mallory and Guy Bullock. This pair virtually by themselves would accomplish what in the long run amounted to a brilliant reconnaissance of Everest. During the following months, the other members puttered off in various directions, performing botanical and topographical missions that had little bearing on finding a route up the mountain.

As always, Mallory's mood swung wildly between giddy enthusiasm and leaden disenchantment. By the beginning of 1921, as he prepared for Everest, now thirty-four years old, he had reached a gloomy crossroads in life. He had quit his teaching job at Charterhouse, with no clear notion of what to do next. Ideally, he would have become a writer, but he lacked confidence, complaining to Robert Graves in a letter from shipboard, "I can't think I have sufficient talent to make a life-work of writing, though plenty of themes suggest themselves as wanting to be written about. Perhaps I shall get a job at a provincial university." At the moment, he was reading that masterpiece by his Bloomsbury admirer, *Queen Victoria:* no doubt Lytton Strachey's sardonic command of prose set a daunting example to Mallory of what a real writer could do.

On June 13, Mallory caught his first sight of Everest—like "a prodigious white fang excrescent from the jaw of the world," as he would write in the expedition book. The distant vision was daunting in the extreme: in a letter to Ruth, he recorded "the most stupendous ridges and appalling precipices that I have ever seen. . . . All the talk of easy snow slope is a myth." Yet while the sight intimidated Mallory, at the same time it captivated him. The man's obsession with Everest can be said to date from that first glimpse, still fifty-seven miles away from the mountain. As he wrote Ruth, during the subsequent days, "The problem of its great ridges and glaciers began to take shape and to haunt the mind, presenting itself at odd moments and leading to definite plans. Where can one go for another view, to unveil a little more of the great mystery?"

Part of Mallory's genius was a deeply analytical grasp of the shape and structure of mountains. Other climbers might be content to stare with field glasses at a single aspect of the mountain, seeking routes; Mallory was eager, in effect, to create a three-dimensional model in his mind. As he wrote in the official report, "Our reconnaissance must aim at . . . a correct understanding of the whole form and structure of the mountain and the distribution of its various parts; we must distinguish the vulnerable places in its armour and finally pit our skill against the obstacles."

As Mallory and Bullock trudged up one snow-struck valley after another, with the monsoon now in full force, the power of that visionary goal drove them across a succession of bleak landscapes. Mallory described one such clime in *Mount Everest: The Reconnaissance:*

> It was a desolate scene, I suppose; no flowers were to be seen nor any sign of life beyond some stunted gorse bushes on a near hillside and a few patches of coarse brown grass, and the only habitations were dry inhuman ruins; but whatever else was dead, our interest was alive.

By June 25, Mallory and Bullock had reached the terminus of the Rongbuk Glacier, the massive ice stream that drains the whole north side of Everest. For a month, the indefatigable duo would explore approaches, only to be stymied and puzzled again and again. Few Europeans had yet traveled on any of the colossal Himalayan glaciers: used to the easy highways such rivers of ice formed in the Alps, the two British climbers were severely frustrated by the jumbled séracs, the crevasse-riddled icefalls, and the weird ice pinnacles, called *nieves penitentes,* that the Rongbuk threw in their path. The glacier was, Mallory wrote, "not a road but an obstacle"; and, "The White Rabbit himself would have been bewildered here." Part of the time, the men hiked in snowshoes, but even so, in the soggy monsoon conditions they often could not avoid wading knee-deep through slush pools.

All the while, Mallory kept staring at the mountain, analyzing it. Early on, he had decided, as he jotted in his diary, "Last section of East arête should go." Here was a pregnant observation, for on that last section of what would come to be called the northeast ridge, Mallory and Irvine would vanish three years hence.

Just as early, Mallory recognized that the key to reaching the northeast ridge was gaining the 23,000-foot saddle of snow and ice that he and Bullock named the Chang La, or North Col. The approach to the col from the main Rongbuk Glacier, however, looked impossible. For weeks, the two men reconnoitered, climbing lower peaks just to acclimatize and to gain new views of Everest, teaching their "coolies" (as they called the porters) the rudiments of mountaineering.

In the course of these explorations, the men climbed to another col on the west of Everest, called the Lho La. From here, the two became the first Europeans to behold the Khumbu Glacier and its upper basin, the Western Cwm (pronounced "Coom"), which Mallory named, slapping a Welsh term for an alpine basin onto a Himalayan landscape. The Khumbu and the Western Cwm would prove the route by which Hillary and Tenzing would make the first ascent of Everest, thirty-two years later. From the Lho La, however, the 1,500-foot drop to the Khumbu unfolded as a "hopeless precipice." The question was moot, in any event, for at the pass, the men stood on the border of Tibet and Nepal, and they were forbidden to enter the latter country.

Always Mallory's eye was fixed on the dotted line his imagination had already drawn from the North Col to the summit. "We saw the North Col quite clearly to-day," he told his diary on July 15, "and again the way up from there does not look difficult."

Thus the immediate task of the reconnaissance was to see if the North Col could be gained from the opposite, or eastern side. Later Mallory, that geographical perfectionist, would castigate himself for not discovering in 1921 that the East Rongbuk Glacier, a tributary ice stream that enters the Rongbuk proper by a V-shaped side valley two and a half miles above the terminus, would prove the royal road to the North Col. (Virtually all modern expeditions to Everest's north side, including Simonson's in 1999, haul their loads up a succession of camps on the East Rongbuk, establishing Camp IV on the North Col.) But that narrow, V-shaped entry of the East Rongbuk into the main glacier is all too easy to miss; and the existing Royal Geographical Society maps Mallory was using argued an entirely different structure of ridges on the northeast side of Everest.

To gain the North Col, then, Mallory and Bullock undertook a heroic end run to the north and east, skirting dozens of nameless subsidiary peaks, until they could find and ascend the Kharta Glacier. Before they could launch that effort—the second great prong of the reconnaissance—during a brief reunion with team leader Charles Howard-Bury, Mallory received some devastating information. The photographic plates he had labored for more than a month to expose, lugging a large camera to distant heights, were all blank, for he had been inserting them backwards. Once more, Mallory's chronic mechanical ineptitude had taken its toll. This "hideous error," as he called it in the expedition report, came as "an extremely depressing piece of news."

Mallory's attitude toward the "coolies" who were his only support in the reconnaissance, and without whom it could not have been undertaken, was a mixture of sympathetic curiosity and the cultural condescension that was endemic in his day. Recognizing the importance of being able to speak the porters' own language, he set himself to learning Tibetan. He shared with them the precious chocolates and nuts he received in the occasional parcel from England that made its way to Base Camp.

Yet, as he watched the porters whom he had taught the basics of ice-craft apply their lessons for the first time, he wryly concluded, "It was not a convincing spectacle, as they made their way up with the ungainly movements of beginners." The sirdar, or head porter, Mallory dismissed in exasperation as "a whey-faced treacherous knave, whose sly and calculated villainy" (a matter of selling food rations for personal profit) threatened to wreck the reconnaissance.

The reunion with Howard-Bury and Raeburn, who had done little to help the expedition, only exasperated Mallory further. "I can't get over my dislike of him," he wrote Ruth of the team leader; and with regard to Raeburn, who had arrived grizzled and weak, "When he is not being a bore I feel moved to pity, but that is not often." The high-strung Mallory had even grown irritated with Bullock, his faithful partner in the reconnaissance. "We had rather drifted into that common superficial attitude between two people who live alone together," he wrote Ruth—"competitive and slightly quarrelsome, each looking out to see that he doesn't get done down in some small way by the other."

In early August, Mallory and Bullock worked their way up the Kharta Glacier. So poor was local knowledge of this terrain that the team started southward on what would have been a wild goose chase, lured by a local tribesman's assertion that Chomolungma ("Mother Goddess of the Snows"), the Tibetan name for Everest, lay five days away in that direction. With his keen sense of direction, Mallory grew skeptical, and a cross-examination revealed that in local parlance, there were *two* Chomolungmas: the tribesman had directed the party toward Makalu, the world's fifth-highest mountain.

On August 7, Mallory fell ill, succumbing to a "weariness beyond muscular fatigue." For several days, Bullock and the porters pushed ahead, while Mallory tried to recuperate, lying in his sleeping bag, agonizing over the thought of Bullock reaching the North Col without him. His veering spirits plunged: at such moments, he wrote later, "I hated the thought of this expedition."

To Mallory's further dismay, it turned out the Kharta Glacier did not head on the slopes of Everest after all: the party would have to find and cross another high pass simply to get to the East Rongbuk Glacier. Finally in mid-August, buoyed by the unexpected addition of another climber, H. T. Morshead, who had hitherto been off on a lowland surveying mission, a rejuvenated Mallory and the steady Bullock crested the Lhakpa La, at 22,500 feet. At last they could see, only three miles away, across easy glacier, the slopes leading up to the North Col from the east. They looked climbable.

By now the monsoon hung so heavy on the Himalaya that it was snowing from eight to ten hours a day. On this interminable expedition, it would turn out to be a major accomplishment simply to reach the North Col, and thus pave the way for a true attempt in some future year. Yet now Mallory's spirits soared wildly, as he anticipated making an assault on the summit in September.

It can be argued that on all three Everest expeditions, Mallory underestimated the mountain. It was a common foible: during the early years, one crack European mountaineer after another misjudged the Himalaya in general. In 1895, Alfred Mummery, the finest British climber of the last quarter of the nineteenth century, a genius in the Alps, had tried to climb 26,660-foot Nanga Parbat with only two teammates and a pair of Gurkha porters. From the mountain, he jauntily wrote his wife, "I don't think there will be any serious mountaineering difficulties on Nanga. I fancy the ascent will be mainly a question of endurance." Treating the massive peak as though it were merely a slightly outsized version of Mont Blanc, Mummery vanished with the two Gurkhas on a reconnaissance of the west face. Their bodies were never found. Nanga Parbat would not be climbed until 1953.

Almost never during subsequent decades would a Himalayan mountain fall to the same expedition that first reconnoitered it (the glorious exception being the French on Annapurna in 1950). In his more judicious moments, Mallory recognized how weak the 1921 party was, how formidable Everest's defenses; but then he would stare again at his dotted line from the North Col to the summit and imagine himself sailing past each easy obstacle . . .

In topping the Lhakpa La, the trio of climbers had found the key to the mountain. But now, snow conditions were so atrocious that the party dared not attempt those three miles separating their farthest push from the North Col. For a full month, they played a demoralizing waiting game.

At last, on September 16, the weather changed, as the monsoon began to peter out. In the meantime, the full team had finally assembled on the Kharta Glacier. Mallory organized a carry that got eleven loads of supplies to the top of Lhakpa La. Four days later, he set out with Bullock and Edward Wheeler, the expedition's chief surveyor, to cross the East Rongbuk and climb to the North Col. By now, it had been four months since the party had set out from Darjeeling on horseback.

All through these latter weeks, Mallory's mood had characteristically swung between joy and despair. In his letters home, sometimes the expedition was "a thrilling business," at others "a fraud." "Our present job is to rub our noses against the impossible," he wrote in a despondent moment. Yet in a hopeful one, he blithely predicted, "It is now only a question of waiting for the weather and organizing our push to the summit."

On the morning of September 24, Mallory, Bullock, Wheeler, and three porters got a late start from the Lhakpa La: only Mallory had slept well the night before. The crossing of the East Rongbuk, however, and the climb to the North Col, was mostly a matter of "straightforward plugging," with the leader cutting about 500 steps in the ice just below the Col. They reached the saddle—that prized and elusive goal Mallory had been gazing at for almost three months—at 11:30 A.M.

The climb had been easy enough, but now the six men stood fully exposed to a bitter gale that tore across the gap: it "came in fierce gusts at frequent intervals, blowing up the powdery snow in a suffocating tourbillon." Wheeler was resolute about turning around at once; Bullock, though exhausted, knew how much the effort mattered to Mallory, and was willing to follow him a little farther. After a shouted discussion, the men staggered a few feet on, leaning against the gale, then "struggled back to shelter" on the lee side of an ice cliff. "The wind had settled the question," Mallory later wrote. Yet he felt in retrospect that he could have climbed another 2,000 vertical feet that day, wind or no wind.

As it was, Wheeler came close to serious frostbite, with his circulation restored in camp only by Mallory's rubbing his feet for hours; and Bullock lagged behind on the descent, stumbling into camp two hours after his friends, completely played out.

Thus ended the reconnaissance of 1921. As the party meandered back toward Darjeeling, Mallory was filled with a sense of failure. "We came back without accident, not even a frostbitten toe," he reported to Geoffrey Winthrop Young, trying to look on the bright side; but in the next breath, "It was a pitiful party at the last, not fit to be on a mountainside anywhere." Young wrote back, telling his protégé that "this end of the world is only using the word *success*," and putting Mallory's extraordinary achievement in the perspective that posterity has since granted it: "I can assure you that the colossal effort of lifting an entirely unsuitable party, at the first attempt, on a single pair of shoulders, not only onto the right line but well up it, against hopeless conditions, forms an episode by itself in the history of mountain exploration, and will only be the more appreciated the more time goes on."

On the voyage back to England, Mallory was burnt out and homesick. "I'm tired of travelling and travellers," he wrote David Pye. "What I want to see is faces I know, and my own sweet home; afterwards, the solemn facades in Pall Mall, and perhaps Bloomsbury in a fog; and then an English river, cattle grazing in western meadows."

There was already talk of another expedition in the spring of 1922. The long summer reconnaissance had convinced Mallory that the only time to go to Everest was in April and May, before the monsoon. He also judged that "it's barely worth while trying again . . . without eight first-rate climbers."

Of a 1922 assault, however, at the moment he wanted no part. "I wouldn't go again next year. . . ," he wrote his sister Avie, "for all the gold in Arabia."

As it was, George Mallory would spend only three months at home before setting out on the second Everest expedition.

DURING THOSE THREE MONTHS, Mallory gave some thirty lectures on Everest, and hurriedly wrote six chapters of the official expedition book. The mountain was never far from his mind, and as he penned the last chapter, called "The Route to the Summit," offering a step-by-step logistical brief for success on Everest, the obsession reclaimed him. At only thirty-five, Mallory was beginning to worry that he was past his climbing prime. And that vision, of the relatively easy stages by which a climber might angle up the north face to the northeast shoulder, then along the ridge to the summit, haunted his domestic hours.

By late winter, the Everest Committee had put together a team for the pre-monsoon season of 1922. Once more the pundits opted for leaders long in tooth and short on technical ability. General Charles Bruce, who had served much of his career in the army in India, was made leader, at the age of fifty-six. Colonel Edward Strutt, who was forty-eight, also an ex-soldier, was drafted as climbing leader. (In the 1930s, Strutt would become infamous as the curmudgeonly spokesman for a wholesale British retreat into climbing conservatism, as he deplored the bold technical breakthroughs being promulgated by Germans, Austrians, and Italians in the Alps, which culminated in the first ascent of the north face of the Eiger in 1938.)

Also on board, and well past his salad days, was Tom Longstaff, who held the record for the highest summit yet attained, when he had topped out on 23,360-foot Trisul, in the Garhwal Himalaya, in 1907. (No higher peak would be climbed for the next twenty-one years.)

In view of his brilliant performance the year before, it may seem odd that Mallory was not made climbing leader in 1922. Knowledge of the man's absentmindedness seems to have dimmed his prospects for an official leadership position. As Longstaff mordantly wrote to a colleague after the expedition, "Mallory is a very good stout hearted baby, but quite unfit to be placed in charge of anything, including himself."

Among the younger team members were Teddy Norton and Howard Somervell, who would prove so staunch in 1924, and Geoffrey Bruce, the general's game but inexperienced nephew. Rounding out the party was George Finch, a remarkable climber who would prove the equal of Mallory on this, his only shot at Everest. Finch had been rejected on spurious medical grounds in 1921, and he would later so alienate the Everest Committee as to preclude any chance of being invited in 1924. Chroniclers attribute much of Finch's difficulties to a vague sense on the committee's part that he had too heartily embraced the more ambitious European ideals of climbing in the Alps; in addition, Finch was not a member of the Alpine Club, and, having been educated in Switzerland, had thus by definition not attended the "right" schools.

In the months leading up to the 1922 expedition, the great debate was over the use of bottled oxygen. Finch, a born tinkerer, was the most avid proponent of using gas; Mallory, with his distrust of all things mechanical, the most ardent opponent, deriding what he called the "damnable heresy" of certain physiologists who theorized that humans would never ascend Everest without supplementary oxygen.

All in all, the 1922 party was many times stronger than the ragtag team of 1921. And at first, everything went like clockwork. Mallory and Bullock's 1921 reconnaissance had been so thorough that it had left only one side of Everest unexplored—the southern approaches, ranging out of forbidden Nepal. Mallory's analysis of the possible routes on the other three sides was so penetrating that the 1922 party needed to waste no further time in exploration.

Moving loads and camps steadily up the East Rongbuk Glacier, with an entourage not only of Tibetan porters but of Sherpas from Nepal, the team reached the North Col by May 13. Only six days later, all the necessary supplies were stocked at Camp IV, ready for a pair of summit pushes. At least two weeks of good weather, and maybe three, loomed before the monsoon would close down the mountain.

The plan called for Mallory, Somervell, H. T. Morshead, and Norton to make a first attempt without oxygen, to be followed, if they were unsuccessful, by Finch and Geoffrey Bruce breathing bottled gas. On May 20, the first quartet set out with porters from the North Col at 7:30 A.M. Every step they climbed probed ground where no one had ever been.

At once the cold assailed all four men. Modern climbers have long been dumbfounded on contemplating the primitive gear and clothing with which Mallory and his partners assaulted Everest in the 1920s. The sense of the inadequacy of that equipage was perhaps the single most powerful perception that struck the five climbers on May 1, 1999, when they beheld Mallory's body at 26,700 feet. It is thus worth pausing to note the passage in *The Assault on Mount Everest, 1922*, in which Mallory narrates the break the four men took at 24,200 feet to put on spare clothes and try to get warm:

For my part, I added a light shetland "woolly" and a thin silk shirt to what I was wearing before under my closely woven cotton coat. As this outer garment, with knickers to match, was practically windproof, and a silk shirt too is a further protection against wind, with these two extra layers I feared no cold we were likely to meet. Morshead, if I remember right, troubled himself no more at this time than to wrap a woollen scarf round his neck.

In general, Mallory's passages in the 1922 expedition book are full of details that, in light of what came to pass two years later, seem eerily to foreshadow the great drama of 1924. On the way up into the unknown that day in 1922, the four men came to a dicey slope where crampons would have been useful. (Modern climbers carry and usually wear crampons all the way to the summit.) Yet the men had left theirs at the North Col. Explains Mallory, "We sorely needed them now. And yet we had been right to leave them behind; for with their straps binding tightly around our boots we should not have had the smallest chance of preserving our toes from frostbite." (The leather boots of Mallory's day were soft and pliable. Modern climbers use plastic or nylon double boots so stiff that tightened straps pose no circulation problem.) The fact that, in 1924, Mallory and Irvine again left their crampons at the North Col bears crucially on their fate.

Similarly, as he described the route to the summit he had scouted for months in 1921, Mallory worried aloud, in the expedition book, about "the possibility of turning or of climbing direct certain prominent obstacles" along the summit ridge. Most prominent of all such obstacles would prove to be the ninety-foot-tall Second Step, at 28,230 feet. Climbing higher on May 20, Mallory could see that step as an unmistakable bump on the skyline far above him.

Not only the cold bothered the men; the thin air made them fuzzy-brained. In a clumsy moment, the rope dislodged Norton's pack, which he had laid in his lap during a rest stop. In Mallory's words:

He was unprepared, made a desperate grab, and missed it. Slowly the round, soft thing gathered momentum from its rotation, the first little leaps down from one ledge to another grew to excited and magnificent bounds, and the precious burden vanished from sight.

With the pack was lost critical extra clothing.

At 2:00 P.M., around 25,000 feet, the tired men stopped to pitch camp. There was no level shelf, and the climbers wasted hours piling up stones to make tent platforms, only to abandon one site after another. Ever since 1922, climbers on the north side have had the greatest trouble establishing Camp V; even for Simonson's party in 1999, this was the camp the climbers dreaded, knowing a night there meant a struggle to catch any sleep.

At last the men got two tents droopily pitched, their floors so sloping that the upper climber in each tent rolled all night on top of the lower. Mallory took stock of his comrades. Worst off was Morshead, whose fingers and toes were in the first stages of serious frostbite. Though Morshead made no complaint, "He was obliged to lie down when we reached our camp and was ev-idently unwell." Mallory himself had frost-nipped his fingers as he cut steps up the slope where the men could have easily walked in crampons, and Norton had a frostbitten ear.

After a nearly sleepless night, the men set out at 8:00 A.M. on the twenty-first, still hopeful of reaching the summit. At once, the debilitated Morshead realized he could go no farther: he pleaded that his teammates continue, while he rested through the day in camp. The cold was even worse than the day before; Mallory had to stop, take off one boot, and let Norton rub his foot back into feeling. The going, across downward-tilting plates of dark shale, was made more treacherous by four to eight inches of fresh snow.

By midday, Mallory knew that he and his partners were going too slowly. At their very best, they were capable of gain-ing only 400 vertical feet an hour (in the Alps, Mallory was used to climbing 1,500 feet per hour without breaking a serious sweat). Their progress would only slow as the air got thinner. A simple "arithmetical calculation" made it plain that night would fall before the men could reach the summit.

Resolving to turn around at 2:15 P.M., the men accepted the mountain's victory. In the expedition narrative, Mallory seems gallantly resigned to defeat: "We were prepared to leave it to braver men to climb Mount Everest by night."

Again, how those words foreshadow! For in 1924, in all likelihood, Mallory and Irvine became those braver men.

At their high point, the three men ate a small lunch of chocolate, mint cake, raisins, and prunes; one of them (whose identity Mallory coyly camouflages in *The Assault on Mount Everest*) produced a pocket flask of brandy, from which each of them took a restorative nip. Then they started down.

With a barometer reading adjusted by a theodolite observation, Mallory fixed his high point at 26,985 feet. In *First on Everest: The Mystery of Mallory & Irvine*, Audrey Salkeld and Tom Holzel argue cogently that the true altitude the three men reached on June 21 was only about 26,000 feet. No matter: it was the highest anyone had yet been on earth.

The prudence of their turnaround would emerge late that afternoon. By 4:00 P.M., Norton, Somervell, and Mallory had regained Camp V. There Morshead declared he was feeling well. The four men roped together, then headed down the 2,000 feet toward Camp IV on the North Col. Mallory took the lead, for, as the strongest of the four men, he readily assumed the tiring task of cutting steps for his partners (a much more awkward task going down than ascending).

Suddenly Morshead, coming third on the rope, slipped on a steep slope. His fall pulled an unprepared Norton, last on the rope, out of his steps, and the two of them pulled Somervell loose. The three plunged helpless toward the void 3,500 feet above the East Rongbuk Glacier.

On the verge of cutting a step, Mallory had time only to drive the pick of his axe into the snow and pass the rope over its head, and time to anticipate one of two outcomes. As he put it in the expedition book, "In ninety-nine cases out of a hundred either the belay will give or the rope will break." Miraculously, neither happened now. The pull came not in one tremendous jerk, but accordion-fashion, as each falling climber absorbed the pull of the one below. Mallory belayed with grim resolve: the rope "gripped the metal like a hawser on a bollard," but the pick held.

Almost never in mountaineering history has one man held three falling companions with nothing more solid than an ice axe belay. The rare instances have become legendary deeds. Mallory's astounding belay has not—in part because he was excruciatingly modest about the accident. In *The Assault on Mount Everest*, he not only avoided identifying the man who slipped, he disguised his own identity as the miracle belayer. The four climbers were tagged only as "the third man," "the leader," etc. Only in a letter to Ruth did Mallory make clear who played which role. Even then, he blamed himself as much as his teammates: "I hadn't realised then how shaky Morshead was and had cut rather poor steps."

Though no one was hurt in the all-but-fatal fall, as they staggered in to Camp IV, at 11:30 P.M., Morshead was ravaged with exhaustion. He had been taking ten-minute rests after feeble two-minute bursts of clumping downward, until Norton and Mallory had to take turns propping him up with a shoulder for his arm and a hand around his waist, all but doing his walking for him.

By the time the four men made it back to Camp III the next day, Morshead's fingers had swollen and turned black with frostbite. The men had also become severely dehydrated. Somervell confessed to downing seventeen mugsful of tea; Mallory guessed the man had drunk even more.

TWO DAYS LATER, on May 24, George Finch set out on a second attempt, using oxygen. Because of the physical conditions of all the other team members, he had only one choice for partner— the plucky Geoffrey Bruce, who had climbed no real mountains before Everest.

Nonetheless, the two men set out full of optimism, telling each other, "Of course, we shall get to the top." Finch believed oxygen would make all the difference.

In the end, the pair's struggle up the north face turned into a fight for their lives. At Camp V, they held on to their tent all night while a gale tried to tear them from the mountainside. They waited out the next day, as the storm dispersed, then, with little food or water left, stretched their sortie into a third day as they headed up. Starting at 6:30 A.M., they passed the high point of Mallory, Norton, and Somervell and added 500 feet to the world altitude record. Oxygen *had* made the difference, for, thanks to the storm, Finch and Bruce were far more worn out as they launched their summit attempt than their four teammates had been on their own thrust on May 20.

The choice to turn around was agonizing for Finch, but it was as canny a decision as Mallory's had been. As Finch wrote in the expedition book, "I knew that if we were to persist in climbing on, even if only for another 500 feet, we should not both get back alive." In the end, Bruce's feet were so badly frostbitten that he had to be sledged part of the way down from the North Col.

Finch and Bruce's gutsy push not only set the new altitude record, to a certain extent it eclipsed the luster of Norton, Somervell, and Mallory's brave attempt four days before. And it convinced Mallory for the first time that bottled oxygen, far from a "damnable heresy," might be the key to climbing Everest.

By June 1, the 1922 expedition had accomplished extraordinary things, reaching 26,500 feet and making known for the first time the secrets of the upper north face. The team had exercised such hubris at the cost of nothing worse than some cases of frostbite (Morshead, the worst afflicted, would lose one toe and six fingertips). Had the expedition now packed up and gone home, as most of its members were inclined to do, the venture would have been hailed in England as a grand success.

But fate was not to let the 1922 party off so easily. As May turned to June, and still the monsoon delayed its arrival, Mallory's obsession turned his thoughts upward once more. He talked his teammates into a third, last-ditch attempt.

As it was, most of them were too worn down even to make another stab. Finch gamely set out, but, unrecovered from his ordeal of May 24–26, tossed in the towel at Camp I.

On June 7, Mallory, Somervell, and teammate Colin Crawford led fourteen porters up toward the North Col. An abundance of new snow had blanketed the slope, but Mallory found the conditions ideal for step-kicking. As the party neared the crest, Somervell led up a gentle corridor. Wrote Mallory, "We were startled by an ominous sound, sharp, arresting, violent, and yet somehow soft like an explosion of untamped gunpowder. I had never before on a mountain-side heard such a sound; but all of us, I imagine, knew instinctively what it meant."

From a hundred feet above the party, an avalanche had

broken loose. The three Englishmen, highest on the slope, and the porters nearest them were swept off their feet and knocked a short distance down the slope, but came to rest and dug themselves out. The porters lower on the slope were caught in the avalanche and hurled over a forty- to sixty-foot ice cliff. Their teammates scrambled down the slope and frantically dug in the avalanche debris below the cliff. Six porters were found dead, more likely from the impact of the fall than by smothering under the snow. The body of a seventh was never found.

Overcome with sorrow, the ten survivors stumbled down to Camp III. Mallory was struck by the Sherpas' forbearance in this tragedy:

> The surviving porters who had lost their friends or brothers behaved with dignity, making no noisy parade of the grief they felt. We asked them whether they wished to go up and bring down the bodies for orderly burial. They preferred to leave them where they were.

As the team trudged out from the mountain, Howard Somervell agonized, "Why, oh, why could not one of us Britishers have shared their fate?" The blame for the accident was loaded onto Mallory's shoulders, not only for pushing the late attempt, but because he had approached the North Col in dubious snow conditions. Tom Longstaff, who had already left Base Camp for home when the accident occurred, was unsparing. "To attempt such a passage in the Himalaya after new snow is idiotic," he wrote a colleague two months later.

In the expedition narrative, Mallory painfully retraced his party's steps toward the disaster, wondering out loud whether he ought to have recognized the danger. "More experience, more knowledge might perhaps have warned us not to go there," he wrote, bewildered. "One never can know enough about snow."

Mallory did nothing, however, to shirk his responsibility, writing Geoffrey Winthrop Young, "And I'm to blame. . . . Do you know that sickening feeling that one can't go back and have it undone . . . ?" For the rest of his shortened life, he harbored a black pool of guilt about the catastrophe. Clare Millikan believes that the chief reason Mallory went back to Everest in

1924 was the idea that success might somehow mitigate the tragedy he had brought upon the seven faithful porters.

MALLORY'S ETERNAL FRIEND AND MENTOR, Geoffrey Winthrop Young, tried to gentle his return, insisting the blame for the accident could not be laid on any man, but on "that shadow of huge, dangerous 'chance,' " and reminding him, "You took your full share, a leading share, in the risk. In the war we had to do worse: we had to *order* men into danger at times when we could not share it."

All this gave Mallory faint comfort. At home, he brooded about the expedition, even as he cast about looking for a new job. In the interim, he undertook a three-month tour of America, lecturing on Everest. The tour was a financial failure, Mallory disliked most of what he saw in the United States, and he was homesick for Ruth and his children. Clare was now seven, Beridge six, John only two. Since Clare had been born, thanks to the war and Everest, Mallory had been home less than half her days.

In the spring of 1923, Mallory landed a job teaching history to working men and women in Cambridge University's extension school. He plunged into this new profession with enthusiasm, commuting between Cambridge and the family home in Holt. During these months, his relationship with Ruth was strained. As evidence, we have only certain ambiguous phrases in the letters. Yet the bedrock loyalty of each for the other was not seriously shaken. In October 1923, he moved his family to Cambridge; there, in Herschel House, he and Ruth set out with a will to furnish and beautify the ideal domicile.

Everest was never far from Mallory's thoughts. Once again, he had been writing chapters for the official expedition book. And the very lectures he gave in America were predicated on explaining to the uninitiated the appeal of trying to reach the highest point on earth, from the famous "Because it is there" quip to more extended—if equally gnomic—rationales, such as these lines from one of his American speeches:

> I suppose we go to Mount Everest, granted the opportunity, because—in a word—we can't help it. Or, to state the matter rather differently, because we are moun-

taineers. . . . To refuse the adventure is to run the risk of drying up like a pea in its shell.

In a thoughtful unpublished essay he wrote about this time, called "Men and Mountains: The Gambler," Mallory faced squarely the question of danger and risk in the mountains. Once more, his words seem eerily to foreshadow the future:

> It is clear that the stake [the mountaineer] risks to lose is a great one with him: it is a matter of life and death. . . . To win the game he has first to reach the mountain's summit—but, further, he has to descend in safety. The more difficult the way and the more numerous the dangers, the greater is his victory.

In closing, Mallory grappled with the inevitability of disasters such as the one that had befallen him below the North Col: "But when I say that our sport is a hazardous one, I do not mean that when we climb mountains there is a large chance that we shall be killed, but that we are surrounded by dangers which will kill us if we let them."

That British mountaineers would return to Everest, if not in 1923, then in the spring of 1924, had become a foregone conclusion. And for all his ambivalence, it seems in retrospect inevitable that Mallory would join the expedition. The mountain had become his destiny.

Only months after he had taken his university extension job, he asked Cambridge to give him half a year's leave on half pay; his alma mater was only too glad to comply. Yet as Mallory faced Mount Everest for the third time, it was not with the joyous anticipation of 1921 or '22, but rather with a dark fatalism. To his Cambridge and Bloomsbury friend Geoffrey Keynes, he confided what he dared not tell Ruth: "This is going to be more like war than mountaineering. I don't expect to come back."

Rescue

CA

It wasn't until 9:00 p.m. on May 8 that the Ukrainians high on the mountain, at the top of the First Step, sent out their distress call over the radio. We didn't monitor the call directly ourselves. At Base Camp, the leader of the Ukrainian expedition, Valentyn Simonenko, would come by our tents every so often to ask how things were going. As the day wore on, he got more and more concerned about his teammates. Then he received the call on his handheld radio, and he told us what had transpired.

The Ukrainians were good climbers—full professionals, to the extent that one can be a professional climber in Ukraine. They were determined to go to the top without oxygen. I don't mean to second-guess them, but that decision inevitably cut their margin of safety. Without oxygen, simple things like tying knots, rigging belays, and performing little bits of technical climbing all become much more difficult.

Compared to us, the Ukrainians had a very rigid way of climbing. Ten days beforehand, they told us, "We're going to the summit on May 8." They had planned their summit push based on a logistical pyramid, with climbers and supplies moving from camp to camp by a predetermined schedule. When May 8 turned out to be the worst day in the last month, they didn't seem to have the flexibility to change their plans.

The three climbers going for the summit that day were Slava, Vasil Copitko, and Volodymyr Gorbach. They got to the top about 1:30 P.M., which was good time, but then their problems began to multiply on the descent, as the storm intensified. It took them much longer to go down than they anticipated. In the end, only Slava—who's an amazingly strong climber—made it back to Camp VI. Somewhere above him, Vasil and Volod had stopped to spend the night out. It was Slava who made the 9:00 P.M. radio call from the First Step.

You don't usually bivouac above Camp VI without serious consequences. Once we learned that Volod and Vasil hadn't made it back to camp, we knew they were almost certainly in trouble.

I give the Ukrainians credit for having other teammates at Camp V, ready to go to the assistance of the summit climbers. By evening, the weather had cleared, but it was very windy up high. Wind makes a huge difference. You can be fit, well hydrated, well fed, and moving efficiently, but the wind will take whatever strength you have right out of you.

On May 9, as the storm cleared, we moved on up to ABC, to be ready to take our part in whatever rescue the situation called for. In the morning, Slava climbed back up from Camp VI to look for his partners. He found Volod alone near the First Step, in really bad shape, probably already suffering severe frostbite. Volod's story was that the previous evening, he just sat down and tried to get through the night, because it was dark, he was terribly cold, and he was exhausted. But Vasil decided to continue the descent alone in the dark. That was still a plausible option, until his headlamp went out. Then the route-finding—especially at the exit cracks, where the northeast ridge merges with the Yellow Band—would have become extremely problematic.

Slava got Volod motivated and shepherded him down to Camp VI. To pull this off, still without oxygen, the day after summitting, and not incur any frostbite himself, makes Slava's performance one of the most phenomenal I've ever seen in the mountains. There's no question he saved Volod's life. But as they descended, they saw no sign of Vasil.

One of the classic mistakes in high-altitude climbing is to separate, as Vasil and Volod did. Look at all the accidents on Denali over the years—almost every time a party separates up high, disaster strikes. I don't know whether the two men really made a calculated decision. But when you separate like that, all of a sudden you go from being able to care for someone else, being part of a team, to focusing on your own well-being.

Slava got Volod down to Camp VI, where he spent the night of May 9. Two other teammates climbed up to VI, to help out. Volod's condition, in the meantime, had gotten worse. He could no longer walk under his own power. So on May 10, his teammates and some Sherpas from an expedition of Georgian climbers made a little seatlike basket out of a rope, to carry Volod in. They carried him the full 3,000 feet down to the North Col, two men on either side of him, rotating the job—another superhuman effort.

Meanwhile, Russell Brice, the experienced New Zealand guide, was organizing the further rescue effort from the North Col. He designated us, the Americans, to be in charge of lowering Volod down the steep ice slopes below the North Col, much more technical terrain than the north face from VI down to IV. Brice chose us, I suspect, because we had the most collective experience in rescue work.

Simo reported on MountainZone that "some expeditions have donated their oxygen and their Sherpas and other expeditions have refused to help at all. One group of Sherpas demanded $200 per person to help with the rescue." Personally, I didn't witness any team refusing to help or Sherpas demanding cash, but that was the scuttlebutt. As Simo wrote, an emergency like Volod's does indeed "bring out the best and worst" in the climbers caught up on the periphery of it.

By the afternoon of May 10, Andy Politz, Jake Norton, Tap Richards, and I had climbed up to the North Col to help. Because the carry down from VI had taken so long, Volod didn't arrive until 10:30 at night. We realized we were going to have to make a triage call, depending on the Ukrainian's condition. Could he afford to spend the night at Camp IV, then go down the next day? Or was his case so critical we had to take him down right away, in the night?

It had been snowing sporadically; now it was dark and cold. We brought Volod into our cook tent, gave him some oxygen and an intramuscular shot of dexamethasone, a powerful stimulant. He was on the verge of being comatose, with a pulse of around 60 and a dangerously low blood pressure of 60 over 20.

And he was howling with pain. He could just barely talk to one of his teammates. Somebody said Volod's feet were frostbitten up to the knees, but that may have been an exaggeration.

It became obvious that we had to get him down in the night. The four of us had everything organized by the time Volod arrived. In a rescue operation like this, one person has to take charge and decide how to rig it, then be the point man who calls the shots. This way, it's simply more efficient.

ON THE 1999 MALLORY & IRVINE RESEARCH EXPEDITION, to use its official title, there were a number of very strong climbers. Andy Politz, Eric Simonson, and Dave Hahn had all climbed Everest before. They were also veterans of dozens of search-and-rescue missions.

Yet by May 10, it had become clear to them that the strongest mountaineer on the team was Conrad Anker—even though he had never been higher than 24,000 feet before. Most of the other members were professional guides. Conrad had done some guiding, but had purposely turned his back on that *modus vivendi*. At thirty-six, nearly two decades after he had started to climb, what motivated him above all else was the chance to put up difficult new routes on little-known mountains among the remote ranges of the world.

By the spring of 1999, Conrad Anker was no household name on the American outdoor scene. He made his living principally as a sponsored climber for the North Face, the equipment firm that had pioneered the practice—novel in the U.S. at the time, though common in Europe—of paying top-notch mountaineers a regular salary to design and endorse North Face products, schmooze with clients, make appearances at retail stores, and climb at the highest level the rest of the time.

Within the North Face stable of sponsored athletes, a rather keen rivalry at times prevailed. To this competition, Anker seemed oblivious. Meanwhile, as he racked up one sterling coup in the mountains after another, celebrating his deeds only in the occasional understated note or article in the *American Alpine Journal*, his reputation among the cognoscenti grew. By 1999, he was recognized as one of the finest three or four exploratory mountaineers in America.

Though he spends most of his down time in Telluride, Colorado, Conrad's heart still resides in the house in Big Oak Flat, California (in the Gold Rush country, just west of Yosemite Valley), where his parents live. His mother, Helga, is German, his father, Wally, an American of mixed German and Scotch-Irish descent. Despite his vagabondage, Conrad remains very close to his parents, whom he calls "my best friends."

"My mother likes to say that I began climbing in the womb," says Conrad—because while she was pregnant with him, her third child, she and her husband hiked the rim of Yosemite. As a child, Conrad tagged along on extended backpacking trips with his family. He feels today that those outings gave him a solid grounding as a mountaineer. "Nowadays a lot of people come to the sport by training in a climbing gym," he says. "They may know how to pull up an overhang, but they don't know what an afternoon cloudburst can do to you if you don't pitch a tarp. I learned that at a ripe young age."

Despite his apprenticeship in backpacking, Conrad did not begin to rock-climb until the relatively late age of eighteen. He showed great promise from the start, leading pitches of 5.7 difficulty (on a scale ranging from 5.0 to 5.14) in sneakers only weeks after he first tied on to a rope. His first expedition was an attempt on Mount Robson, the majestic and dangerous peak in the Canadian Rockies: "We failed miserably."

In 1987, the American Alpine Club gave Conrad a $400 Young Climber's Grant to pursue an expedition to the Kichatna Spires, arguably Alaska's most jagged and daunting low-altitude mountains. With three companions, he made a five-day first ascent of the southeast face of Gurney Peak, thus entering the elite of American mountaineers capable of pulling off cutting-edge climbs in major, bad-weather ranges.

Meanwhile, Anker desultorily pursued his education, finally graduating from the University of Utah at the age of twenty-six, with a degree in commercial recreation—"basically hotel and resort management," he explains. "I didn't go straight through. I took every spring off for an expedition, and I worked to help pay for college."

Like most passionate climbers, Conrad in his twenties chose jobs not with a view toward career potential, but according to how much freedom they gave him to take off at the drop of a hat—"anything," he clarifies, "that I could work at, save up some money, then quit to go climbing." In this fashion, he paid the bills for five years by working construction. During college, he had tended the counter at the North Face store in Salt Lake City, selling carabiners and Gore-Tex jackets—his initial connection with the company that would later pay him to climb.

A brief sortie into entrepreneurship—with a climbing buddy, Conrad started Alf Wear, a two-man firm peddling fleece hats and river shorts—left him dissatisfied. He credits his father, a bank examiner, with giving him a crucial push. "My father told me to go climbing, to make the most of it, because you can always sell hats when you're sixty-five. So I sold the company for $10,000, which seemed like big bucks at the time."

Freed to pursue his passion, Conrad developed into not only a first-rate mountaineer, but an exceedingly diversified one. Most climbers focus on a specialty: pure rock-climbing, alpine walls, expeditions to 8,000-meter peaks in the Himalaya. Conrad has excelled in all the branches of the mountaineering art. By now, for instance, his résumé includes numerous one-day ascents of eight different routes on El Capitan, in Yosemite, normally the province of rock-wall specialists who barely know how to hold an ice axe. Yet Conrad has also pulled off fiendishly difficult climbs on the "Big Three" Patagonian towers, Cerro Torre, Torre Egger, and Cerro Stanhardt; soloed serious new routes in the frozen wastes of Antarctica; and put up elegant first ascents on such formidable mountains as Latok II in the Karakoram of Pakistan and Mount Hunter in Alaska.

Anker's sometime partner, photographer, and veteran mountaineer Galen Rowell hails this versatility: "Conrad can ski down virgin faces of big peaks in subzero Antarctica, climb El Cap routes in a day for fun, sport-climb 5.12, speed-climb up Khan Tengri in the Tien Shan faster than the Russian Masters of Sport, climb the north face of Everest or Latok, ice-climb the wildest frozen waterfalls, run mountain trails forever, plus enjoy hanging out with his friends talking about other things besides mountains."

The formative influence on Conrad as a climber, the one partner who served as a true mentor, was Terrance "Mugs" Stump, whom Conrad met in 1983, climbing outside of Salt Lake City. More than ten years Conrad's senior, Stump was already a legend, known for visionary ascents in the great ranges, often performed solo, with no self-publicizing fanfare whatsoever (he did not regularly write notes for the climbing journals). Stump had been a star defensive back for Joe Paterno at Penn State, had played in the Orange Bowl, but had wrecked his left knee playing football. He discovered his true métier only in his late twenties.

"He was really motivated to become a true climber," remembers Conrad. "He'd say, 'You can't sell out, guiding bumblees up glorified ski runs. You've got to do real climbing, you've got to climb this and this and this, that's where it's at.' "

Conrad quickly progressed from protégé to equal partner. "Nietzsche has a passage in which he talks about the 'ball of knowledge.' We wouldn't be where we are as human beings if it weren't for the collective knowledge that's passed on from one generation to the next. It was like that with Mugs and me. He had this ball of energy and knowledge. Some days he would pass the ball to me, and I would climb better than he, and other days he wanted it back. We were really well paired, we had the same sense of humor, and he set me on the path to becoming a professional climber."

For four years, Mugs and Conrad lived together in Sandy, a suburb of Salt Lake, in a house provided them by John Bass (nephew of Dick Bass, the first man to climb the Seven Summits, or highest points on all the continents), who had the remarkable idea of supporting American mountaineering by giving promising climbers such as Stump and Anker a helping hand.

Mugs and Conrad climbed together often, ranging from Yosemite to Alaska. Their "epic" occurred on the Eyetooth, a savage pinnacle of ice and granite southeast of Denali. A ferocious storm kept the two men trapped on a portaledge—an artificial tent platform hung from pitons over the vertical void—for seven days and nights. "We ran out of food," recalls Conrad. "We probably could have rappelled off, but Mugs was into hanging, so we just relaxed and stayed there till the storm was over."

Stump had come of age during the time before American climbers could live off sponsorship. He became a professional climber only by guiding nearly full-time. Rather than settle into the rut of guiding the same trade route over and over, like the standard walk-up on Rainier or the West Buttress on Denali, Stump took ambitious clients onto less-traveled routes. It was on one such outing, in 1992, descending Denali's South Buttress, that Stump, scouting a crevasse that blocked the path, had the upper lip collapse beneath him. He was buried under tons of debris, his body never found.

Mugs's death was perhaps the most devastating setback of Conrad's life. In a sense, he has never gotten over the loss. Much of his resolve not to make a living as a guide springs from Mugs's "pointless" accident on an easy route, as he tended clients. "On Everest this year," says Conrad, "the day we packed up Base Camp was the seventh anniversary of Mugs's death. I took all the leftover juniper from the *puja*, half a gunny-sack-full, and torched it up into one big billowing cloud."

Like all serious mountaineers, Conrad has had his share of close calls. The closest came in 1991, on Middle Triple Peak in the Kichatna Spires of Alaska. Conrad and longtime pal Seth Shaw had made the second ascent of the mountain's splendid east buttress and were completing the descent. With only eighty vertical feet remaining between them and the glacier, Shaw reached the bottom of his rappel and prepared to clip in to the anchor Conrad had set up two feet away. Just as he reached out a carabiner to clip, the snow platform on which he had come to rest broke loose. Shaw was still on rappel, at the end a 300-foot rope doubled through the anchor on the pitch above. Climbers customarily tie knots in both ends of the rappel rope, so they don't slide off the end by accident; normally the snow ledge breaking would have been inconsequential.

"We were just exhausted," remembers Conrad. "We'd been on the route five days. We'd gone into the Kichatnas super-light, with only fourteen days' food, and this was our twenty-first day. Somehow I tied a knot in one end of the rope and not in the other."

Thus as Shaw's weight came on the single knot, it pulled

the rope through the anchor above, like a line whipping unchecked through a pulley. Shaw fell eighty feet and landed hard on the glacier.

"I thought he was dead. So here I am in the Alaska Range, with no radio, the nearest other human being sixty miles away, eighty feet up, with no rope. I thought, Oh, my God, how do I get out of this?"

All Conrad had to extricate himself from a hopeless predicament was a small "rack" of climbing gear, a few cams and nuts and five or six pitons. He began to place what gear he could in marginal cracks in the vertical wall and aid-climb his way gingerly down. He had to put his weight on one insecure piece, transfer it to the piece below, then remove the upper cam or nut to reuse as he got lower. At all times he tried to keep three interconnected pieces affixed to the rock. "It was like trying to cross a desert," he says, "with twenty feet of railroad track that I had to keep pulling up from behind and resetting in front.

"I started hearing voices. Human voices, but I couldn't tell what they were saying. It's the eeriest thing I've ever experienced in my life. Eventually, Seth came to and got up. Amazingly, he wasn't even badly hurt. We talked to each other. He was wallowing around in the snow. There was still nothing he could do for me. He didn't have enough gear to lead back up to me with the rope, and besides, he was utterly exhausted.

"I just kept shuffling gear, cleaning ice out of the crack, trying to keep three pieces in at all times. Then suddenly I slipped and the whole thing blew—all three pieces came out at once."

Conrad fell most of the eighty feet, his back slamming against the rock, then his head. Yet the glacial snow on which he landed saved him, as it had Shaw, from death. Conrad's back rang with excruciating pain (the injury still occasionally bothers him, eight years later), but the two men now faced a thirty-mile ski out to Rainy Pass with no food. The desperate jaunt took them thirty-six hours. Along the way, they found a hunting cabin; inside, they gorged on a jar of peanut butter and bags of salt and pepper (laid in to season the slabs of fresh moose meat hunters might lug there the next October). Glad to be alive, they crossed the Happy River and reached a roadhouse hunting lodge at Rainy Pass, where their bush pilot picked them up.

The professional turning point in Conrad's life came in 1993, when North Face signed him on as a sponsored climber. His first contract earned him a relative pittance, but by living frugally and supplementing his take with the odd carpentry job, he made ends meet. By 1999, Conrad was making a decent income from his North Face gig, although going to Everest entailed so many missed obligations that—just like Mallory in 1924—he agreed to take a cut to half pay.

As a North Face representative, Conrad travels around the country, giving slide shows, taking potential clients out for a day of easy skiing or climbing, or giving a climbing demonstration on an artificial wall. He can be sardonic about the work, which he sometimes alludes to as "the petting zoo." Yet, in his habitually earnest way, he waxes enthusiastic about his encounters with a public avid to taste adventure, even if vicariously.

"I can use my slide shows and ski outings as a chance to share my outlook on life, which is fundamentally Buddhist," he says. "People come to see slides of me climbing, to share my adventures, but I can use the opportunity to talk about being a good person, about how anger and hatred disrupt an expedition, about how sometimes it takes a little more effort to be positive than negative, but that it's ultimately life-enriching. I'd like to take what notoriety or fame comes my way and turn it into something good, as for instance Sir Edmund Hillary has, building schools and hospitals in Nepal. I'd like to share what mountains have done to change my life, and become a spokesperson for goodness."

Anker's partner on many extreme climbs during the last seven years, Alex Lowe, says, "More than anyone I've traveled and climbed with, Conrad reaches out to the people around him, giving of himself, his time, and his illimitable energy. No one who comes in contact with him walks away unaffected."

At thirty-six, Conrad stands six feet two and weighs 175 pounds, though he lost a few pounds on Everest. His sandy hair is usually unkempt and tousled, as if the wind had rioted in it, and a day's growth of beard often furs his cheeks and chin. His manner is soft-spoken and unfailingly polite, though his blue-green eyes hold his interlocutor with an unblinking gaze. Even at rest in his own apartment, his body seems to have the catlike grace, coiled ready to spring, of a great athlete in great shape.

In the wake of Mugs Stump's death, mired in a year-long depression, Conrad taught himself to paint with watercolors. This sedentary occupation has become his one serious hobby, which he pursues even in the midst of expeditions. His deft landscapes have a kind of Japanese simplicity. He gives away every painting he executes, and never signs them.

On Everest, with his fascination for all things Buddhist, Conrad became intensely curious about the lives of the yak herders who carted the expedition's 16,000 pounds of food and gear from Base Camp to ABC, about the lives of the Sherpas who would make such invaluable colleagues up high. "Because the United States is so recently settled, despite the Native Americans," he says, "in our country we don't really have a mountain culture. In places like Tibet, I'm completely fascinated with the mountain cultures that have been at home in the great ranges for centuries."

Good climbers, on the whole, are not often deeply empathic men or women. Their own agendas of triumph and vindication loom too large. Conrad Anker is an exception. And just as his sympathetic openness led him to spend hours lounging with the yak herders, without being able to exchange an intelligible word, it was not surprising that, when the Ukrainian Volod Gorbach lay near death in the middle of the night on the North Col, Conrad should unhesitatingly take charge of the difficult and dangerous evacuation that might save his life.

CA

WE PUT VOLOD INTO A SKED—a sled litter that looks something like a big plastic burrito—with foam pads underneath him. We put his harness on, tied the harness to the top of the sled, put him inside a sleeping bag, and wrapped him up so he wouldn't fall out of the sled. There were the four of us Americans—Tap Richards, Jake Norton, Andy Politz, and me—along with Silvio, a very strong Italian climber.

We knew there were fixed ropes in place all the way down

the steep section below the North Col, and thus fixed anchors about every 150 feet. We had a 600-foot rope of our own, so we could make a good long lower, then rappel down the fixed ropes ourselves.

Tap and I stayed at the top, lowering Volod. We used a Munter hitch, a simple knot that would cinch down on the rope even if we lost control of it altogether. The rope came up from Volod's sled, through a belay device attached directly to the anchor, then to Tap and me. It's as if we were lowering him through a pulley, with an emergency brake backing us up.

Andy and Silvio were rappelling the fixed lines, but tending the sled, one on either side of it. They had short leashes to the top and bottom of the sled, to make sure it didn't flip upside down, which can easily happen in a lower if the foot of the sled fetches up on a ledge or a bulge. Jake went first, to set up each station for the next maneuver.

As soon as we'd lowered him the full 600 feet, Andy and Silvio would tie Volod off. Tap and I would cut loose the ropes and rappel quickly down; by the time we got to the next station, Volod was rigged for the next lower. We were doing all this in the dark, with headlamps, communicating with each other by radio.

As smoothly as we managed the lowering, the sled was still bouncing off corners and shelves in the ice, causing Volod a lot of pain, though your body will kick in with endorphins that act as natural painkillers. We could see that his nose was frostbitten—black and shriveled up, with bits of flesh coming off. We knew his feet and hands were frostbitten, but we didn't want to take off his gloves or boots.

I'm proud to say that we were really efficient. We did five 600-foot lowers in only an hour and a half. Some of them were tricky: the second went over an open crevasse, the fourth down a really steep ice chute.

By midnight, we'd gotten Volod to the foot of the North Col. It was as dark and cold as it was going to get. There was still a considerable horizontal carry to ABC, at 21,000 feet. Russell Brice had organized a team to take over from us there, comprised of Dave Hahn and Thom Pollard from our party, several climbers from other expeditions, and a whole bunch of cook boys and Sherpas, about twenty people in all. They took Volod's sled and carried him across the relatively flat part of the glacier incredibly fast. They just flew. Part of the way, they could slide him on another rescue sled, which Simo had arranged to get to the foot of the lower.

In his sled, Volod kept trying to sit up. The guys who were carrying him said, "Just twenty minutes. Twenty more minutes!" Volod could barely whisper in response. They finally got him to ABC at 2:30 A.M.

There, Russell Brice had converted his dining tent into a medical ward. They had a heater going to keep Volod warm. The Ukrainian team doctor put some oxygen on Volod and got some fluids into him. He could barely manage to drink through a straw. Finally they took off his gloves and boots. The hands and feet weren't completely black, but they looked bad. What nonplussed me was to see that on the lower part of his body, Volod had only long underwear on, then fleece pants, then Gore-Tex pants. No down suit on his lower body.

That serves as a reminder of just how important mountaineering is in certain impoverished Eastern European countries. Not only Ukraine, but Russia, Poland, Czechoslovakia, Slovenia—all those countries have produced superb Himalayan climbers, who've succeeded without even being able to afford proper equipment, let alone having the luxury of being sponsored. There's a tremendous amount of national pride involved in their efforts. It emerges from the Ukrainian expedition brochure, written in fractured English, but eloquent all the same:

> The Ukraine needs herous to entering to the XXI Centure, and they are forged there, where the maximum concetration of phusical, mental and intellectual forces is necessary for achievement the purpose. There is no better place, than climbing to the highest summits of the world.

On the morning of the eleventh, I built a carrying basket out of two metal pack frames, some duct tape, and some parachute cord, and five Tibetans carried Volod the thirteen miles down to Base Camp. He wasn't in great shape, but he was lucky to be alive.

We had never worked better as a team than during this

rescue. Dave Hahn put up a nice acknowledgment of our achievement in his MountainZone dispatch:

> As I recall from normal life, heroes are seldom seen up close and personal. In fact, where I work at Mount Rainier, I have to drive all the way down to the big city, buy a ticket and a $6 beer, and sit way up in the stands in the hopes that Ken Griffey Jr. will smack one over the wall and give me a long-distance look at greatness. Here, I just look over my tea cup and see heroes every day.

Two months after the expedition, I got word from a Ukrainian team member, Roman Coval, in Kiev. Volod had had the last joints of two fingers on his left hand amputated, as well as several toes on both feet. It could have been a lot worse.

He hoped to climb again. As Roman rather mordantly put it, "In Ukraine, we have enough climbers without fingers or toes—the only problem is to change boot size."

The team had received special honors from the president of the Ukraine. The expedition, Roman said, had been "highly approved by the government."

No one ever found any trace of Vasil Copitko. His teammates think that as he tried to descend in the dark late on May 8, he must have fallen off the eastern face of the ridge, above the Kangshung Glacier. If he'd fallen down the north face, above the Rongbuk, somebody later in May would probably have found something. It's entirely possible that Vasil's body will never be discovered.

Despite our success, the rescue had a sobering effect on our team. The Ukrainians weren't novices; they were good, strong climbers who knew what they were doing. Only some minor miscalculations, and the bad luck of weather, put them on the edge of survival. We all knew the same thing could happen to us.

It was May 11, and no one except the three Ukrainians had yet summitted on Everest from the north. We had been planning to use these days to rest up for our second search and our summit attempt. Instead of gathering strength and fattening up, here we were, exhausting ourselves performing a rescue in the middle of the night.

I tried to recuperate on May 11, but it wasn't a very restful day. On the twelfth, we went back up to the North Col. I figured I was as ready as I'd ever be. My mind had fixated on an image of the Second Step, which I'd seen only in pictures. If I could climb it free, I could judge how hard it would have been for Mallory to have climbed it on June 8, 1924.

Teeth in the Wind

DR

MALLORY'S GRIM PREMONITION came true: in the end, the 1924 expedition was more like war than mountaineering.

Yet as he sailed from England to India, then as he rode and hiked toward Everest, Britain's finest climber was filled not with foreboding, but with optimism. "I can't see myself coming down defeated," he wrote Ruth from the remote Tibetan village of Shekar Dzong. To his former teammate Tom Longstaff, he predicted, "We're going to sail to the top this time, and God with us—or stamp to the top with our teeth in the wind."

As he had in both 1921 and '22, once more Mallory underestimated Everest. His bravura performance two years before, along with Finch's, had made the summit seem well within his grasp. At times, his certainty about success could approach cocksure arrogance, as during his lecture tour of America, where, envisioning a third expedition, he boasted, "Mount Everest is asking for trouble." Yet at other times, his confidence was laced with threads of doubt, as in a sentence he wrote his sister Mary from shipboard, "Anyway, we've got to get up this time; and if we wait for it and make full preparations, instead of dashing up at the first moment, some of us will reach the summit, I believe."

The 1924 party was even stronger than the 1922 team had been. General Charles Bruce was back as leader, now fifty-eight and in poor health even before the expedition started. But Howard Somervell and Teddy Norton were returning, seasoned by their previous Everest foray. The cool-headed Norton was appointed climbing leader, despite Mallory's greater experience and technical ability. Somervell brought along Bentley Beetham, a young climber of whom much was expected, for in the summer of 1923, the pair had had a season in the Alps few other Englishmen could match, climbing some thirty-five peaks in six weeks.

Noel Odell imported vast funds of exploratory wisdom and alpine expertise, and though he was slow to acclimatize, once he was in shape, he would outperform all his teammates except Norton and Mallory. Odell's Spitsbergen protégé, Sandy Irvine, was an unproven quantity, but quickly showed that his solid athleticism and buoyant spirit could make up for lack of mountaineering experience. Rounding out the party were Geoffrey Bruce, now a mountaineer, thanks to his 1922 campaign; John de Vere Hazard, a fast and experienced climber in the Alps; and photographer-cinematographer John Noel, who would prove staunch in a supporting role.

Mallory thought the team "a really strong lot," and Norton went even further: "I doubt if so strong a party will ever again be got together to climb Mount Everest."

During the journey to the mountain, Mallory badly missed his wife, to whom he wrote often and at great length. The sense of having done her harm, during whatever "difficult time" the couple had gone through the previous autumn, afflicted him. "I fear I don't make you very happy," he wrote from the ship. "Life has too often been a burden to you lately, and it is horrid when we don't get more time and talk together." For Ruth, her husband's absence was a constant ache: "Dearest one, I do hope you are happy and having a good voyage. I am keeping quite cheerful and happy, but I do miss you a lot."

On the approach, General Bruce recurringly felt "seedy" and weak. Unable to keep up with his teammates, he chose a low-altitude detour to get himself to the village of Kampa Dzong two days after the main party. Before he could reach that town, however, he collapsed in a full-blown malarial fever, apparently the flaring up of a long-dormant infection. Bitterly disappointed, he resigned from the expedition and returned to India.

Teddy Norton was made leader of the party, and Mallory

climbing leader (which he would have been de facto in any case). Fortunately, the two men got along splendidly, even during the expedition's lowest moments, and made no important decisions without consulting each other.

Mallory's obsession had taken the form of trying to come up with a perfect plan for linked parties to push for the summit. John Noel noted that "he seemed to be ill at ease, always scheming and planning." By April 14, still far from the mountain, he had devised a strategy, which he detailed enthusiastically in a letter to Ruth; then, only three days later, he was seized with what he called a "brain-wave" that presented him a new plan like an epiphany. Essentially it boiled down to putting a pair of parties simultaneously in position to go to the top from different camps. From Camp IV on the North Col, two climbers with fifteen porters would climb to Camp V, build four tent platforms, and descend. Another pair, the first, "gasless" summit party, would occupy Camp V one night, then push on with eight porters, skipping Camp VI, to set up a Camp VII at 27,300 feet—higher than anyone had yet been on earth. At the same time the second summit party, using oxygen, would establish a Camp VI some 800 feet lower than Camp VII. "Then the two parties," wrote Mallory to Ruth, "start next morning and presumably meet on the summit."

The plan looked good on paper, and Norton was won over by it; but of course on Everest the best-laid schemes of men and mountaineers "gang aft a-gley." In the end two parties would indeed try for the summit, one without oxygen, one with, but they would launch four days apart, and by the time the second pair—Mallory and Irvine—set out for the top, the first pair had stumbled down to Camp III. The visionary Camp VII, perched high on an exposed shoulder just below the crest of the northeast ridge, would never be established.

As the team members had sailed for India, a nagging worry plagued their thoughts. The disaster of 1922, when seven porters had died, would still be fresh in the Sherpas' minds: would any volunteers be willing to go back up on the mountain that had proved so deadly? The team was thus overjoyed when they learned through their trading agent that a "number of Sherpas, Bhotias, and hill-men generally" had come in, hoping to be hired.

Yet Mallory and his comrades were right to anticipate the Sherpas' terrors. In 1924 it would take very little to demoralize the porters altogether. A foretaste of their ambivalence came in the behavior of Angtarkay, who had been dug out of the avalanche debris in 1922. "We felt bound to take him on again," wrote General Bruce in the opening chapter of *The Fight for Everest* (which he was proud to pen, despite having given up the expedition), "but he soon broke down, and returned with me." In Bruce's view, the Sherpa had never "really recovered from that terrific experience" of being buried alive in snow.

Mallory's paramount vow was to avoid a recurrence of the 1922 tragedy. As he wrote his sister Mary on May 2, in another passage that resonates with ironic foreshadowing, "No one, climber or porter, is going to get killed if I can help it. That would spoil all."

With some seventy porters, cooks, and "domestic servants" in tow, the expedition rode on ponies through Tibet. An omen of bad fortune, however, awaited them at the Rongbuk Monastery. There they learned that the head lama was ill and could not perform the *puja* on which the porters set such store to keep them safe on the mountain. And there, the climbers beheld a fresh mural painting chillingly memorializing the 1922 accident: in Bentley Beetham's words, it depicted "the party being pitch-forked down the mountain-side by hoofed devils and sent spinning into the colder hell."

Two weeks later, during a lull in the foul May weather that thwarted the expedition, Norton marched the whole team back down to the monastery. Instead of a blessing, however, the head lama offered the Englishmen a malediction. "Your turning back brings pleasure to the demons," he intoned in Tibetan, which an interpreter translated to John Noel. "They have forced you back, and will force you back again."

For all this, as he reached Base Camp, armed with his "brain-wave" scheme, Mallory was still awash in the highest optimism. "I can't tell you how full of hope I am this year," he wrote his sister Mary. "It is all so different from '22, when one was always subconsciously dissatisfied because we had no proper plan of climbing the mountain."

All during the journey to India and the march across Tibet, Mallory had been sizing up Sandy Irvine. From the start, as he wrote Ruth, he found the Oxford undergraduate "sensible and not highly strung," though he could not resist an impish sketch of Irvine as "one to depend on for everything except conversation." Later, during a storm on the mountain, Mallory read poems out loud from his cherished anthology, Robert Bridges's *The Spirit of Man*. Somervell was surprised to learn that Emily Brontë had written poems as well as novels; Odell was stirred by the last lines of Shelley's *Prometheus Unbound;* while "Irvine was rather poetry-shy, but seemed to be favourably impressed by the Epitaph to Gray's 'Elegy.' " (One wonders just how that gloomy meditation in a country churchyard on the anonymous dead resonated with the twenty-two-year-old: "The paths of glory lead but to the grave.")

Norton too was taken with Sandy Irvine's quiet strength. In *The Fight for Everest*, he described his young teammate thus: "Irvine, as befitted a rowing blue, was big and powerful—with fine shoulders and comparatively light legs." Irvine was a little heavier than Mallory, and in superb shape, having rowed two seasons for the Oxford crew that beat Cambridge in 1922 for the first time since 1913. Though not as classically beautiful as Mallory, he was a remarkably handsome young man. A family tradition records that at Oxford, Irvine became a womanizer, conducting an affair with his best friend's stepmother. He had a very fair complexion, whence his nickname; on Everest, Irvine would suffer more than anyone else from sun- and windburn.

Herbert Carr, Irvine's biographer, who knew him at Oxford, thought the youth innately shy. "He had an odd way of laughing," Carr remembered. "It was a silent laugh, visible but not audible, a long low reverberating chuckle which lit up his face with sunny merriment. And as his normal expression was grave, the contrast was all the more striking."

Irvine was born in Birkenhead into genteel circumstances not unlike Mallory's. He attended Shrewsbury public school, then Merton College at Oxford. His academic fortes were chemistry and engineering; in French and Latin, on the other hand, he was woefully weak. Even in adolescence, he was extraordinarily adept at tinkering and inventing. While still at Shrewsbury, he sent the blueprints for two machines of his devising to the War Office—an interrupter gear for firing machine guns through propellers, and a gyroscopic airplane stabilizer. Both had already been anticipated by Hiram Maxim (the inventor of the machine gun), but the flabbergasted War Office, according to Herbert Carr, sent him "most warm congratulations . . . with instructions to go on trying."

In Mürren, in Switzerland, at Christmas 1923, Arnold Lunn, who conceived the slalom race, gave Irvine skiing lessons. "He is the only beginner I have ever known," reported Lunn, "who brought off at his first attempt a downhill Telemark." After only three weeks of practice, Irvine entered and won the Strang-Watkins Challenge Cup (a slalom race) against seasoned veterans. He loved the sport, writing Lunn in gratitude, "When I am old, I will look back on Christmas, 1923, as the day when to all intents and purposes I was born. I don't think anybody has ever lived until they have been on ski."

Intensely competitive, on the approach to Everest Irvine found good sport in challenging Mallory to a pony race. The older man was charmed by the self-confident youngster. After several weeks on the East Rongbuk Glacier, Mallory noted that Irvine "has been wonderfully hard-working and brilliantly skilful about the oxygen. Against him is his youth (though it is very much for him, some ways)—hard things seem to hit him a bit harder. . . . However, he'll be an ideal companion, and with as stout a heart as you could wish to find."

Mallory was genuinely dazzled by Irvine's aptitude with the oxygen gear. After the young man had taken the apparatus apart, stripped some four pounds of useless metal from each set, and put the pieces back together, Mallory marveled, "What was provided was full of leaks and faults; and he has practically invented a new instrument." For someone as mechanically inept as Mallory, Irvine's facility was nothing short of miraculous: watching his comrade tinker with the ill-designed equipment, he was like a tone-deaf auditor listening in uncomprehending admiration to the playing of some twenty-two-year-old Mozart.

Ever since 1924, observers have second-guessed Mallory's decision to take Irvine along on the summit push, rather than the far more experienced Odell. Many have wondered whether Irvine's meager skills in the mountains could have contributed to the fatal accident. Walt Unsworth, in his definitive history of Everest, went so far as to speculate whether Mallory "had formed a romantic attachment for the handsome young undergraduate."

One need not reach so far for an explanation. Once Mallory had committed himself to the use of oxygen on his summit attempt, Irvine's expertise became critical. Odell was ostensibly in charge of the oxygen apparatus, but he was a withering skeptic about its benefits. Mallory clearly explained his reasons in a letter to Ruth: not only was Irvine the oxygen expert, but if Mallory paired with Odell, that would leave an all-too-inexperienced duo of Irvine and Geoffrey Bruce as backup.

> And so Irvine will come with me. He will be an extraordinarily stout companion, very capable with the gas and with cooking apparatus. The only doubt is to what extent his lack of mountaineering experience will be a handicap. I hope the ground will be sufficiently easy.

Irvine kept a diary on Everest, making his last entry only the day before setting out with Mallory for the top. The diary was retrieved by Odell and published in 1979. It is a fairly stolid document, written for the most part in the pronoun-less staccato so often favored by the unintrospective: "Spent afternoon repacking Primus stoves, also negotiating to buy pony. . . . Put lightening fasteners on my sleeping bag." Irvine wastes little breath on observing his teammates; a kind of tunnel vision dominates his perspective. Like many another Englishman on his first trip to Asia, he was a bit squeamish. In one Tibetan village, "I was very impressed by the dirtiness of the whole place, and also the smell." In another: "Went this afternoon to see Tibetan Devil dancers—this most weird performance was continuous from 2:00 P.M. to 6:30 P.M., and got rather monotonous towards tea-time."

Somehow during the approach, Irvine received dismaying news from Oxford. "Got wire to say that Cambridge won by 4½ lengths—incredible!" A day later, he had not absorbed the shock: "I still can't get over Oxford being beaten by four and a half lengths—I should like to have details of the race."

Yet the diary captures Irvine's obsessive tinkering, as he records one attempt to fix a piece of equipment after another. The balky oxygen gear became his greatest challenge. A typical passage:

I spent all afternoon and evening again patching up oxygen apparatus. Out of box No. 2023 I made up two complete instruments (1A and 2A), but without emergency tubes, as all in this box leaked—either the pipe or the brass of the union was porous. Number 3A had a dud flowmeter which I took to pieces—it appeared corroded inside around the bottom bearing. I cleaned this up as well as I could, but it is still sticky at $1\frac{1}{2} + 3$, but works alright if hit every now and then. Number 4A had a blocked reducing valve, so was turned into MkIII pattern.

One can imagine Irvine trying to explain these arcane matters to a puzzled Mallory. Indeed, a kind of unintentional humor emerges from the diary, as Irvine tends to the gear woes of (in Longstaff's pithy characterization from 1922) the "stout hearted baby" who was "quite unfit to be placed in charge of anything, including himself." A sample:

APRIL 11th. . . . I mended Mallory's bed, Beetham's camera, Odell's camera tripod and sealed up a full tin of parrafin. . . .

APRIL 12th. Spent day in camp, did some photography, sorting biscuit boxes and doing a job of work on Mallory's camera, which spun out and took all afternoon.

APRIL 19th. . . . I spent this afternoon mending one of Mallory's ice axes (broken by a coolie). . . .

APRIL 27th. . . . After about an hour Mallory came in with a box of crampons, and I spent till dinner time fitting crampons to Mallory's and my boots, and trying to fix them without having a strap across the toes, which is likely to stop the circulation.

APRIL 28th. . . . Spent most of the afternoon with Beetham's camera, also mending my sleeping bag and Mallory's saddle.

All this compulsive puttering, of course, was of immense practical value to the expedition. Irvine might be "poetry-shy," but he

would be irreplaceable high on the mountain when gear mal-
functioned.

As the expedition progressed, the bond between Mallory
and Irvine grew. After May 7, in Irvine's diary, Mallory is called
"George"; the others remain Norton, Somervell, Hazard, and so
on. The friendly competitiveness that had dictated a pony race
extended onto Everest, where, however, Irvine could never keep
up with his older friend, that wizard of motion in the mountains. "When we moved on," Irvine wrote on May 4, "a devil
must have got into Mallory, for he ran down all the little bits of
downhill and paced all out up the moraine. It was as bad as a
boat race trying to keep up with him."

THE PARTY REACHED BASE CAMP beneath the terminus of the
Rongbuk Glacier on April 29. At once, the members started
sorting out 300 yak-loads of gear to be carried to subsequent
camps on the East Rongbuk. Mallory's optimism had reached
full bore: he had already decided that May 17, give or take a day
or two, would be the summit day; and he predicted to Ruth,
"The telegram announcing our success . . . will precede this letter, I suppose; but it will mention no names. How you will hope
that I was one of the conquerors!"

Then everything started to go wrong. The weather was
fiercely cold and stormy even at the comparatively low altitude
of Base Camp. On April 28, "a bitterly cold wind blew, the sky
was cloudy, and finally we woke up to find a snowstorm going
on. Yesterday was worse, with light snow falling most of the
day." The team tried to impose English cheer on their desolate
camp, feting their arrival with a five-course meal and several
bottles of champagne.

By now, the number of porters and yak herders had swelled
to 150. With Gurkha leaders who were veterans from 1922, these
natives set out on April 30 without sahibs, singing and joking, to
establish Camps I and II. The plan was for half to turn back after
dumping their loads at I, with the other half pushing on to II the
next day. But on their way back to Base Camp, night caught the
porters, and only twenty-two of the seventy-five arrived. They
were found the next day unharmed; but their disappearance had
launched a devastating series of porter problems that would crip-
ple the expedition in the following weeks.

On May 7, carrying loads to Camp II, the porters ran into such atrocious weather that Mallory ordered them to leave their loads a mile short of camp. Meanwhile another contingent of porters had been trapped at Camp III, at 21,500 feet, "with only one blanket apiece," as Geoffrey Bruce wrote in the expedition book, "and a little uncooked barley to eat, and were now driven out unable to bear it longer, utterly exhausted." When they staggered down to II, they swelled a crowd of porters to twice the number for whom there was tent space. There was no choice but to break open the food and tents intended for higher on the mountain.

At Camp III, Mallory and three teammates endured temperatures as low as –22° F. with high winds. If conditions were this bad low on the mountain, they would be unendurable above the North Col.

Mallory had hoped to establish Camp IV on the North Col by May 9, but that day Odell and Hazard were turned back in a blizzard only three quarters of the way up, dumping their loads in the snow. The men spent a wretched night at III, later described by Bruce:

> The blizzard continued with unabating violence, and snow drifted into our tents covering everything to a depth of an inch or two. The discomfort of that night was acute. At every slightest movement of the body a miniature avalanche of snow would drop inside one's sleeping-bag and melt there into a cold wet patch.

In these conditions, the porters' morale plunged alarmingly. Mallory and his companions did everything they could to exhort the natives to further efforts, but it was a losing battle. No doubt the failure of the men to receive the lama's *puja* at the Rongbuk Monastery contributed to their apathy, as did the frightful weather. Mallory blamed an "Oriental inertia": "They have this Oriental quality that after a certain stage of physical discomfort or mental depression has been reached they simply curl up. Our porters were just curled up in their tents." But he had to admit that the sahibs themselves had also curled up to wait out the storms: they spent "most of the time in the tents— no other place being tolerable."

At last Norton bowed to the inevitable, ordering all the porters and climbers to retreat all thirteen miles back to Base Camp. The column formed, in Bruce's word, "a melancholy procession of snow-blind, sick, and frost-bitten men." Even in retreat, disaster struck, as one porter fell and broke his leg, another developed a blood clot on the brain, and a cobbler had "his feet frost-bitten up to the ankles." The latter two died shortly after, to be buried near Base Camp.

The Englishmen were faring little better, with ailments ranging from hacking coughs to "glacier lassitude." Mallory had weathered intestinal problems so severe it was suspected that he had appendicitis. Beetham was laid low by sciatica so persistent that he would never climb very high on the mountain.

In 1922, the team had reached the North Col by May 13, and Mallory, Somervell, and Norton had launched the first summit attempt only seven days later. During the corresponding week in 1924, the party had failed even to reach the North Col. Instead, they spent six days at Base Camp, licking their wounds. Mallory wrote Ruth, "It has been a very trying time with everything against us."

Not until May 17—the day Mallory had originally plotted for the summit—did the debilitated climbers head back up the mountain. Somervell later judged that the appalling week of waiting out storms at Camp III had "reduced our strength and made us . . . thin and weak and almost invalided, instead of being fit and strong as we had been during the 1922 ascent."

Nonetheless, Mallory rallied his waning optimism, fixing May 28 as his new summit date, and wrote Ruth with dogged hope, "It *is* an effort to pull oneself together and do what is required high up, but it is the power to keep the show going when you don't feel energetic that will enable us to win through if anything does."

At last, on May 20, Mallory, Norton, Odell, and one Sherpa gained the North Col. Mallory took the lead up a steep ice chimney that formed a difficult but safe alternative to the slope that had avalanched in 1922. Norton left a vivid description of that 200-foot lead: "You could positively see his nerves tighten up like fiddle strings. Metaphorically he girt up his loins. . . . Up the wall and chimney he led here, climbing carefully, neatly, and in that beautiful style that was all his own."

The ascent, wrote Mallory, was "a triumph of the old gang." Yet on this expedition where nothing seemed to go right, a further catastrophe struck the four men as they descended.

It began as Mallory decided to head down by the ill-starred 1922 route. Early on, the men hit slopes where they needed the crampons they had left at Camp III. Mallory chopped occasional steps, but following unroped, first Norton slipped, then the Sherpa—both fortunately stopping after short slides. Leading downward, Mallory suddenly plunged ten feet into a hidden crevasse. As during his fall on the Nesthorn in 1909, when, belayed by Geoffrey Winthrop Young, Mallory never let go of his axe, now he showed remarkable self-possession even in mid-plunge. As he wrote Ruth, "I fetched up half-blind and breath-less to find myself most precariously supported only by my ice-axe, somehow caught across the crevasse and still held in my right hand—and below was a very unpleasant black hole."

Mallory shouted for help, but his teammates, caught up in their own perils, neither heard him nor knew what had happened. Eventually he "got tired of shouting" and managed to excavate a delicate sideways passage out of the crevasse—only to find himself on the wrong side of it. "I had to cut across a nasty slope of very hard ice and, further down, some mixed un-pleasant snow before I was out of the wood." The four men re-gained Camp III thoroughly exhausted.

Even so, they had finally reached the North Col, the plat-form from which all summit attempts must be launched, and the weather showed signs of ameliorating. The ice chimney Mallory had so deftly led presented a logistical obstacle to porters getting loads to the col, but fixed ropes eased the pas-sage, and eventually Irvine wove a rope ladder and hung it on the chimney, turning the pitch into a reasonable scramble for laden men.

Then, just as hope glimmered in Mallory's breast, yet an-other dire predicament thwarted the team's progress. On May 21, Somervell, Irvine, and Hazard led twelve porters up to the North Col. While Somervell and Irvine descended, Hazard and the porters remained at Camp IV, awaiting the arrival of Bruce and Odell, who planned to use the porters to push on to estab-lish Camp V. But a snowstorm began that evening and contin-ued through the next day, while the temperature again dropped to –22° F. Odell and Bruce never left Camp III. The next day, Hazard decided to descend with the porters.

Among the expedition members, Hazard was distinctly the odd duck. A loner, he was not well liked by his teammates. As Somervell later wrote, Hazard "built a psychological wall round himself, inside which he lives. Occasionally, he bursts out of this with a 'By Gad, this is fine!' . . . Then the shell closes, to let nothing in."

Now, as he led the porters down the slope made treacherous with new snow, Hazard failed to notice that four of them balked and returned to their tents at Camp IV. When Hazard showed up at III with only eight porters, Mallory was furious. "It is difficult to make out how exactly it happened," he wrote; "but evidently he didn't shepherd his party properly at all."

This was perhaps too harsh a judgment, as the demand that one man be responsible for twelve porters in marginal conditions was a well-nigh impossible one. What the fiasco meant, however, was that four porters, no doubt terrified and possibly suffering frostbite, were stranded above all the sahibs on the mountain.

On May 24, Somervell, Norton, and Mallory headed up to rescue the porters. Norton judged the situation so desperate that, as he later wrote, "I would have taken a bet of two to one against a successful issue to our undertaking." Norton and Somervell were off form, but "Mallory, who on these occasions lived on his nervous energy, kept urging us on." Above the ice chimney, the snow slopes were loaded, ready to avalanche. With the other two belaying from the last safe stance, Somervell led a diagonal traverse, using every bit of the 200 feet of rope the men had carried. He ran out of line some ten yards short of the crest of the col. The porters, having heard the men approach, peered nervously over the edge. It was 4:00 P.M.—dangerously late.

Norton, who spoke Tibetan, coaxed the porters into trying the ten-yard descent to Somervell on their own. Two men made it safely, but the other two fell, slid and tumbled, then came to rest in precarious spots a short distance from Somervell. With no other option, he drove his axe into the slope, untied, fed the rope over the axe shaft, and, simply holding the end of the rope in his hand, sidled toward the trembling porters. With hardly an inch to spare, he grabbed each by the scruff of the neck and hoisted them back to the anchored axe. The worn-out men regained Camp III long after dark.

This debacle demoralized the porters utterly. After May 24, only fifteen of the fifty-five porters were of any use at all. The team dubbed these stalwarts "Tigers," a hortatory epithet that has been current on Everest ever since. In the meantime, however, the party was in such disarray that Norton had no other choice than to order once more a wholesale retreat. By May 25, the team had limped all the way down to Camp I, at 17,900 feet.

"It has been a bad time altogether," wrote Mallory to Ruth on May 27, in the last letter she would ever receive from him. "I look back on tremendous effort and exhaustion and dismal looking out of a tent door into a world of snow and vanishing hopes."

AT HIS MOST PESSIMISTIC, Mallory had never foreseen a rout as complete as the one Everest had dealt his team during the preceding month. Less plucky men might have packed up and gone home at this juncture, with less than a week of May remaining. Instead, the 1924 expedition held what they called a "council of war."

Neither food nor oxygen had yet been carried to Camp IV; only tents and sleeping bags were stocked there. Norton's revised plan was to forget altogether about oxygen, in hopes that two light, fast parties of two men each, supported by porters, could make leaps on three successive days to Camps V and VI and then to the summit. The plan, of course, was pie in the sky, for as yet no climber had taken a single footstep above the North Col.

Both Somervell and Mallory had developed racking coughs. Mallory described his to Ruth: "In the high camp it has been the devil. Even after the day's exercise . . . I couldn't sleep, but was distressed with bursts of coughing fit to tear one's guts—and a headache and misery altogether."

Yet Norton offered Mallory a place in the first pair, arguing that "though he had so far borne the brunt of the hardest work, yet the energy and fire of the man were reflected in his every gesture." His partner would be Geoffrey Bruce, who at the moment, Mallory wrote, was "the only plumb fit man" in the party.

At last the weather relented, granting the team several "cloudlessly fine and hot" days in a row. Despite their ailments, the climbers moved efficiently up the mountain. Mallory had no illusions about the team's thin chances of summitting: "It is fifty to one against us, but we'll have a whack yet and do ourselves proud," he wrote Ruth. Yet he closed his last letter with a jaunty vow: "Six days to the top from this camp!"

On June 1, for the first time, climbers set off upward from the North Col, as Mallory, Bruce, and eight porters intended to establish Camp V at 25,300 feet. The day was again sunny, but above the col a bitter wind out of the northwest swept the face. Some 300 feet short of their goal, the porters flagged. Four of them had to drop their loads and head down, while the other four stumbled up to the stony slope where Mallory had already begun to build makeshift tent platforms. In a heroic effort, Bruce and Sherpa Lobsang ferried the other four loads up to camp. In doing so, however, Bruce exhausted himself; it was later determined that he had "strained his heart," and after June 1, he was of little use on the mountain.

That night the two sahibs and three porters slept at V. In the morning, Mallory was ready to push on, but Bruce was too weak to climb, and the porters had, in Norton's phrase, "shot their bolt." There was no choice but to head back down to Camp IV.

There Odell and Irvine were installed in a supporting role, cooking meals for the summit pair and carrying oxygen up to them as they descended. Irvine chafed at his role, writing in his diary, "I wish I was in the first party instead of a bloody reserve." But during the previous week, he too had been unwell: he had had a three-day bout of diarrhea, and on May 24 he recorded, "felt very seedy." The sunburn that had afflicted his fair complexion for more than a month had gotten worse. The men had brought various ointments, including zinc oxide, to smear their faces with, but these remedies apparently did Irvine little good. As early as April 11, he had written, "My face is very sore from wind and sun . . . and my nose is peeling badly."

On May 24, he noted, "face very sore indeed." By June 2, the sunburn was in danger of incapacitating the staunch young man. That night he wrote, "My face was badly cut by the sun and wind on the Col, and my lips are cracked to bits, which makes eating very unpleasant."

A day behind Mallory and Bruce, Norton and Somervell formed the second summit party. Rather than appoint himself to this team, which would seize the apparent last chance for the summit, Norton had asked Mallory and Somervell to determine who Somervell's partner should be. From among Odell, Irvine, Hazard, and Norton, they had nominated Norton. It would prove a wise choice.

Norton and Somervell left the North Col with six carefully selected Tigers on June 2. Still the weather held. They carried their own tent and sleeping bags, for if the plan had worked, Mallory and Bruce would at the moment be pushing on to establish Camp VI, and all four Englishmen would need tents and bags at both V and VI.

In *The Fight for Everest*, Norton gives a detailed description of the clothing he wore that day—a state-of-the-art wardrobe for 1924. It makes for a startling contrast with the down suits and plastic boots of today's Everest climber:

> Personally I wore thick woollen vest and drawers, a thick flannel shirt and two sweaters under a lightish knicker-bocker suit of windproof gaberdine the knickers of which were lined with light flannel, a pair of soft elastic Kashmir putties [ankle wraps, the predecessors of modern gaiters] and a pair of boots of felt bound and soled with leather and lightly nailed with the usual Alpine nails. Over all I wore a very light pyjama suit of Messrs. Burberry's "Shackleton" windproof gaberdine. On my hands I wore a pair of long fingerless woollen mits inside a similar pair made of gaberdine; though when step-cutting necessitated a sensitive hold on the axe-haft, I sometimes substituted a pair of silk mits for the inner woollen pair. On my head I wore a fur-lined leather motor-cycling helmet, and my eyes and nose were protected by a pair of goggles of Crookes's glass, which were sewn into a leather mask that came well over the nose and covered any part of my face which was not naturally protected by my beard. A huge woollen muffler completed my costume.

Neither man wore crampons, for despite Irvine's tinkering, no one had yet figured out a way to strap these invaluable spikes to one's boots without cutting off circulation to the feet.

On the way up, Norton and Somervell were dismayed to meet one of Mallory's Sherpas descending. From him, they learned of the first party's turnaround, then crossed paths with their friends as they despondently clumped down to the North Col. Continuing with only four porters, Somervell and Norton reached Camp V at 1:00 P.M., where they settled in to cook and get warm.

Lower on the mountain, the men had cooked on Primus stoves using liquid fuel; above the North Col, however, they preferred Unna cookers that burned a solid cake of Meta fuel made in France. The chore of making dinner was one all the men detested. As Norton put it, "I know nothing—not even the exertion of steep climbing at these heights—which is so utterly exhausting or which calls for more determination than this hateful duty of high-altitude cooking."

Scooping pots full of snow to melt, heating the water to its tepid boiling point at altitude, filling Thermos flasks with hot water or tea for the morrow, washing up the greasy pots—and then, "Perhaps the most hateful part of the process is that some of the resultant mess must be eaten, and this itself is only achieved by will power: there is but little desire to eat—sometimes indeed a sense of nausea at the bare idea—though of drink one cannot have enough."

In the morning, the men did not get off until 9:00 A.M., so difficult was it for Norton to persuade three of the four porters to continue. "I remember saying, 'If you put us up a camp at 27,000 feet and we reach the top, your names shall appear in letters of gold in the book that will be written to describe the achievement.' "

Despite the late start, the climb on June 3 went smoothly enough; the weather was still fine, with even less wind than the day before. Somervell's cough gave him so much trouble he had to stop now and then. Even so, the two Englishmen passed their own 1922 high point of 26,000 feet just after noon, and later they exceeded Finch and Geoffrey Bruce's mark of 26,500 feet. Sending the three porters back, Somervell and Norton pitched Camp VI at 26,800 feet, once again shoring up a tent platform by piling loose stones. They were higher than human beings had ever been on earth.

After a month of demoralizing setbacks, of ignominious defeat staring them in the face, the two men dared believe that the summit might be within their grasp. Norton slept well, Somervell tolerably. "Truly it is not easy to make an early start on Mount Everest!" Norton would write. Yet on June 4, the men were moving by 6:40 A.M.

After an hour, the pair reached the foot of the broken cliffs that would come to be known as the Yellow Band. They had topped 27,000 feet, with the summit about 2,000 feet above them. Moving diagonally up and right, Norton and Somervell found easy going on ledges that led one to the next.

It was here that Norton purposely diverged from the ridge route that had always been favored by Mallory. To his eye, a long, gradually ascending traverse toward what would come to be called the Great Couloir afforded the best line on the upper north face. The day remained perfect, though the men climbed in bitter cold.

Yet now, with the top tantalizingly close, the men began to succumb to the awful ravages of altitude. Somervell's cough had grown alarming, necessitating frequent stops. Norton had made the mistake of taking off his goggles when he was on rock: at 27,500 feet, he started seeing double. Without oxygen, the men were slowed to a crawl. "Our pace was wretched," Norton later wrote. He set himself the goal of taking twenty steps without a rest, but never made more than thirteen: "we must have looked a very sorry couple."

By noon, however, the two men were approaching the top of the Yellow Band. They were some 500 or 600 feet below the crest of the summit ridge, well to the west of the First Step. All at once, Somervell announced that he could go no farther, but he encouraged his partner to continue alone. With weary, careful steps, Norton pushed on, traversing farther right along the top of the Yellow Band. He turned two corners, the second directly below the skyline feature the team had named the Second Step—"which looked so formidable an obstacle where it crossed the ridge," Norton presciently wrote, "that we had chosen the lower route rather than try and surmount it."

Beyond the second corner, the going abruptly got worse, as

the slope steepened and the downsloping "tiles" underfoot grew treacherous. Twice Norton had to backtrack in his steps and try another approach. Still he pushed on, at last reaching the Great Couloir.

There, suddenly, he waded through knee- and even waist-deep unconsolidated snow. In a moment, the full terror of his predicament came home to him:

> I found myself stepping from tile to tile, as it were, each tile sloping smoothly and steeply downwards; I began to feel that I was too much dependent on the mere friction of a boot nail on the slabs. It was not exactly difficult going, but it was a dangerous place for a single unroped climber, as one slip would have sent me in all probability to the bottom of the mountain. The strain of climbing so carefully was beginning to tell and I was getting exhausted. In addition my eye trouble was getting worse and was by now a severe handicap.

Norton turned around. He was only 300 yards west of Somervell, and 100 feet higher, but, as often happens when a climber acknowledges defeat, a kind of mental collapse now seized the man. As he approached his partner, facing a patch of snow thinly overlying sloping rocks—ground he had walked easily across perhaps half an hour before—he lost his nerve. Norton pleaded for Somervell to throw him a rope. Once tied in, he accomplished the crossing.

The expedition would later fix Norton's high point as 28,126 feet—only 900 feet below the summit of the world, which stands 29,028 feet above sea level. Unless Mallory and Irvine reached a greater height four days later, Norton's altitude record would stand for the next twenty-eight years. His oxygenless record would last twenty-six more, until Peter Habeler and Reinhold Messner summitted without gas in 1978.

Starting down at 2:00 P.M., the men stayed roped together all the way back to Camp VI. Along the way, Somervell dropped his ice axe and watched as it bounded out of sight. At VI, he replaced it with a tent pole.

By sunset, the men, now unroped, had reached Camp V. Rather than spend a miserable night on one of its sloping, inadequate tent platforms, the duo pushed on down into the dusk, aiming for Camp IV. And here, Somervell nearly lost his life. Glissading ahead, Norton noticed that his partner had stopped above. All during the expedition, Somervell had painted skillful watercolors of the scenery (a number of the paintings were published in *The Fight for Everest*). His thinking addled by altitude, Norton now guessed that his friend had stopped to make a sketch or painting of the mountains bathed in their twilight glow. In fact, Somervell's worst coughing fit so far had seemed to lodge some object in his throat that threatened to choke him. At last he coughed it loose in an explosion of blood and mucus. It was later determined that Somervell had coughed up the lining of his larynx.

As Norton staggered down to the North Col in the last light, Mallory and Odell came up to meet him and guide him through the crevasse-riven shelf just above camp. One of the men shouted that he was bringing an oxygen cylinder. Norton yelled back, again and again, in a feeble wail, "We don't want the damned oxygen; we want drink!"

So MIGHT THE 1924 EXPEDITION have ended, with an extremely gallant stab by Norton and Somervell that had established a new world altitude record. The monsoon would be upon the mountain any day now. Yet as he regained the North Col, Norton learned that Mallory had decided, in the event of the second attempt failing below the summit, to make one last push—with oxygen. After descending himself from Camp V on June 2, Mallory had organized a porter carry from Camp III that had wrestled a quantity of bottles up to the North Col. Norton expressed his approval; privately, he "was full of admiration for the indomitable spirit of the man." He demurred only in wishing Mallory had chosen Odell for his partner rather than Irvine.

In the middle of the night of June 4–5, Norton woke up with a terrible pain in his eyes, to find that he had gone snowblind. He could do nothing the next day to help his friends organize their assault except talk to the porters in their own language. The key to communicating with these vital allies above Camp IV on the two previous attempts had been Norton's and Bruce's competence in their language. Mallory had a "smattering of Hindustani," but Irvine spoke scarcely a word of any tongue the Sherpas understood.

At 7:30 in the morning of June 6, Norton said goodbye to the summit pair. "My last impression of my friends was a handshake and a word of blessing." Still blind, he could not watch the men move off among the snow humps and crevasses toward the north face. Later that day, Norton went down to Camp III, so helpless that six porters had to take turns carrying him along the moraine. During the next four days, wrote Norton, "we were to pass through every successive stage of suspense and anxiety from high hope to hopelessness," until Camp III would eventually lodge in his memory as "the most hateful place in the world."

Noel Odell, the sole climber left fit enough to serve in support, would spend eleven days at or above the North Col, a performance, as Norton later put it, with "no equal in our short record of high climbing." Odell too was full of admiration for Mallory's indomitable will. As was characteristic of the man, Odell bore his own exclusion from the summit party with serene magnanimity.

Despite their ailments, using oxygen Mallory and Irvine had come up from Camp III to IV on this last push in only two and a half hours—a time that some of the strongest climbers in the 1990s would be proud of. Up till the last minute, Irvine had fussed with the oxygen sets, jury-rigging final adjustments.

His spirit must also have been indomitable, for he cannot have gotten much sleep during his last nights on the North Col. The final diary entries reveal just how badly Irvine was suffering from his sunburn. On June 3: "A most unpleasant night when everything on earth seemed to rub against my face, and each time it was touched bits of burnt and dry skin came off, which made me nearly scream with pain." June 5, on the eve of departure: "My face is perfect agony."

Despite having slaved for more than a month to improve the oxygen apparatus, Irvine told Odell that "he would rather reach the foot of the final pyramid without the use of oxygen than the summit by means of its aid! He thought that if it were worth while doing at all, it was worth while doing without artificial means." Such a purist sentiment would scarcely be voiced again for the next fifty years.

At 8:40 A.M. on June 6, using oxygen, with eight lightly burdened porters going without, Mallory and Irvine left the North Col. Odell took a picture of the two: by his own admission a hurried snapshot, the men's features unrecognizable as they putter with gear, it has nonetheless been reprinted hundreds of times over, for it is the last photo taken of either man—unless there are images lying dormant in the celluloid inside Mallory's Vestpocket camera, lost somewhere still on Everest.

A clear morning deteriorated into a cloudy day with evening snow. At 5:00 P.M., four of the porters returned from the north face, with a note from Mallory, ensconced in Camp V: "There is no wind here, and things look hopeful."

The next day, as planned, Odell and a Sherpa climbed to Camp V. Soon after they got there, the remaining four porters descended from above, bringing another message, this one from Camp VI at 26,800 feet:

Dear Odell,—

We're awfully sorry to have left things in such a mess—our Unna Cooker rolled down the slope at the last moment. Be sure of getting back to IV to-morrow in time to evacuate before dark, as I hope to. In the tent I must have left a compass—for the Lord's sake rescue it: we are without. To here on 90 atmospheres for the two days—so we'll probably go on two cylinders—but it's a bloody load for climbing. Perfect weather for the job!

> Yours ever,
> G. Mallory

To the end, Mallory was dogged by his forgetfulness and mechanical ineptitude. The loss of the cookstove was ominous, for unless the men had already filled their Thermoses with water or tea before it "rolled down the slope," they would be hard put to melt any snow for breakfast or to carry on the climb. Not having a compass (Odell in fact found the instrument in the tent at V) would be less consequential on summit day, unless the pair were engulfed in a white-out. The "90 atmospheres," Odell knew, amounted to a flow of about three quarters of the rig's capacity. At that rate, each bottle ought to have lasted at least four hours. If the men carried two cylinders apiece on June 8, they should have been able to climb for eight hours breathing gas.

With the message to Odell was the one to John Noel, exhorting the men lower on the mountain to start looking for Mallory and Irvine "either crossing the rock band under the pyramid or going up the skyline at 8.0 p.m." Odell read this note, assuming at once, as all historians have, that Mallory meant 8:00 A.M. on June 8.

After sending the five Sherpas down, Odell spent a peaceful night alone at Camp V. The sunset transported him, as he gazed in three directions at distant peaks sharply etched in the clear air, including the massive sprawl of peaks surrounding Kangchenjunga, the world's third-highest mountain, 100 miles to the east. "It has been my good fortune to climb many peaks alone and witness sunset from not a few," he later wrote, "but this was the crowning experience of them all, an ineffable transcendent experience that can never fade from memory."

Odell started out to climb to Camp VI at 8:00 A.M. on June 8. The day had dawned clear, but by mid-morning "rolling banks of mist commenced to form and sweep from the westward across the great face of the mountain." The wind, however, was light. The day seemed propitious for a summit climb. "I had no qualms for Mallory and Irvine's progress upward from Camp VI," Odell reported, "and I hoped by this time that they would be well on their way up the final pyramid."

Still climbing without oxygen, Odell was by now so completely in his element that, rather than take the shortest approach to Camp VI, he wandered about the north face, appraising its geology, discovering his beloved fossils. Just after noon, he climbed the "little crag" at 26,000 feet, stared at the skyline ridge, and made his legendary sighting. There, some 2,000 feet above him, he watched as the lead figure quickly climbed to the top of a step on the ridge, then waited as the second figure followed, both men "moving expeditiously as if endeavouring to make up for lost time." Then the clouds moved in again, blocking his view.

It was 12:50 P.M., five hours later than the 8:00 A.M. appearance Mallory had seemed to predict in his note to John Noel. Odell now felt a mild alarm, but he listed to himself all the reasons that could have contributed to his friends' delay.

(Curiously, few commentators in the last seventy-five years have wondered whether Mallory's 8:00 A.M. prediction might have simply been the final example of his underestimating the mountain. No party had yet managed to leave a high camp on Everest before 6:30 A.M., and the skyline ridge lay more than 1,200 feet above Camp VI.)

In the midst of a snow squall, Odell reached VI at 2:00 P.M. There he was disappointed to find no note from Mallory chronicling the pair's departure, and further disturbed to see pieces of oxygen apparatus strewn about the tent. Yet he would not conclude from the debris that Irvine had made desperate last-minute repairs; instead, he rationalized that his protégé might simply have "invented some problem to be solved even if it never really had turned up! He loved to dwell amongst, nay, revelled in, pieces of apparatus and a litter of tools."

Odell did not notice that Mallory had left his flashlight in the tent—yet another instance, and a potentially weighty one, of his absentmindedness. The flashlight would be rediscovered by members of the 1933 Everest expedition, who turned on its switch and found that it still functioned nine years after it had been left there.

Hoping to find his friends on their way down and guide them back to Camp VI, Odell climbed another 200 feet in dense clouds, whistling and yodeling to signal his presence. Then, realizing that it was too early to expect the pair's return, he made his way back to Camp VI. Just as he got there, the squall ended and the mountain cleared again. Now, however, Odell could see nothing, although warm afternoon light bathed the mountain's upper slopes.

He lingered until 4:30 P.M., then, in obedience to Mallory's note, started back down the mountain, not before leaving Mallory's compass, which he had retrieved from Camp V, in "a conspicuous place in the corner of the tent by the door"—less, one suspects, to enable his friends to navigate down to the North Col than as a charm against the fates. Odell reached Camp V at 6:15 P.M., then, glissading much of the way, descended the 2,300 feet to the North Col in the astonishing time of thirty minutes.

Among the Englishmen, there was only Hazard there to greet him. The others, still weakened by their ordeals of the last few days, were convalescing at Camp III. On the evening of June 8, everyone stared for hours at the upper slopes of Everest, hoping to see the beam of a flashlight or even the flaming burst of one of the emergency flares the porters had carried to Camp VI; but they saw nothing. Still rationalizing away his fears, Odell hoped that moonlight reflected off summits to the west might have aided his friends' descent.

All next morning, Hazard and Odell swept the mountain with field glasses, detecting no signs of life. Unable to bear this idle vigil, at noon Odell started up the north face again with two Sherpas. The well-rested Hazard did not even consider joining him, for he had reached his limit at 23,000 feet.

The three men reached Camp V that afternoon, then spent a sleepless night as a nasty wind threatened to tear the tents loose. On the morning of June 10, with the wind still fierce and cold, the two Sherpas were incapable of continuing. Odell sent them back down to the North Col, then set out alone to climb to Camp VI. For the first time, he breathed bottled oxygen in hopes it would aid his performance, but, true to his ingrained skepticism, turned off the apparatus partway up and "experienced none of those feelings of collapse and panting that one had been led to believe ought to result." Lugging the useless contraption on his back, Odell marched on up to VI, reaching it at midday.

Odell's own account does not dwell on the terrible shock of his discovery. In the most understated fashion, he mentions simply that "I found everything as I had left it: the tent had obviously not been touched since I was there two days previously." Dumping the oxygen set, he at once pushed on above to search for some trace of his companions, even as the weather deteriorated.

In a state of heightened awareness that the dawning tragedy had spurred in him, Odell was now granted something like a revelation:

> This upper part of Everest must be indeed the remotest and least hospitable spot on earth, but at no time more emphatically and impressively so than when a darkened atmosphere hides its features and a gale races over its cruel face. And how and when more cruel could it ever

seem than when balking one's every step to find one's friends?

Odell struggled on for almost two hours, finding nothing. Back at Camp VI, he crawled into the tent to take shelter from the gnawing wind. Then, during a lull, he dragged two sleeping bags up to a precarious snow patch above the tent and laid them out in the form of a T. Four thousand feet below, looking with field glasses, Hazard saw the prearranged signal and knew the worst.

At last Odell closed up the tent and headed down. As he took one more look at Everest's distant summit, his revelation of the utter inhumanity of the great mountain reached a spiritual pitch:

> It seemed to look down with cold indifference on me, mere puny man, and howl derision in wind-gusts at my petition to yield up its secret—this mystery of my friends. What right had we to venture thus far into the holy presence of the Supreme Goddess. . . ? If it were indeed the sacred ground of Chomolungma—Goddess Mother of the Mountain Snows, had we violated it—was I now violating it?

In that freighted moment, chilled to the soul by the mountain's indifference, Odell all at once heard the siren's song:

> And yet as I gazed again another mood appeared to creep over her haunting features. There seemed to be something alluring in that towering presence. I was almost fascinated. I realized that no mere mountaineer alone could but be fascinated, that he who approaches close must ever be led on, and oblivious of all obstacles seek to reach that most sacred and highest place of all. It seemed that my friends must have been thus enchanted also: for why else should they tarry?

Lower on the mountain, Odell's teammates had passed these last few days in an agony of ignorance. In hopes of curing his throat problems, Somervell had descended all the way to Base Camp. On June 11, he wrote in his diary, "No news. It is ominous." And the next day, after several comrades had arrived with their tidings: "There were only two possibilities—accident or benightment. It is terrible. But there are few better deaths than to die in high endeavour, and Everest is the finest cenotaph in the world."

By June 12, the whole expedition had gathered at Base Camp. Wrote Norton later:

> We were a sad little party; from the first we accepted the loss of our comrades in that rational spirit which all of our generation had learnt in the Great War, and there was never any tendency to a morbid harping on the irrevocable. But the tragedy was very near; our friends' vacant tents and vacant places at table were a constant reminder to us of what the atmosphere of the camp would have been had things gone differently.

The men might accept the loss of Mallory and Irvine, but they could not resolve the mystery of what had happened to them. As they retreated from Mount Everest, they speculated ceaselessly as to how their friends had met their end. For the rest of their lives—John Noel the last to die, just short of his one hundredth birthday—they would continue to wonder and speculate, turning over and over like potsherds the fragmentary clues they had to base their guesses on.

The Second Step

CA

By May 15, six of us had reoccupied Camp V, at 25,600 feet. We had two separate agendas: to go for the summit and to conduct a second search. It wasn't predetermined who would do which. Tap Richards, Jake Norton, and I were motivated to climb the mountain, because we hadn't been on Everest before.

In the end, Thom Pollard and Andy Politz volunteered to make the second search. Andy was willing to forgo the summit because he'd climbed Everest and because he'd gotten caught up in the search. Irvine's body and the all-important camera still remained to be found. Thom was not, strictly speaking, part of Simo's team: he'd been hired by *NOVA* to shoot video and take digital pictures, so he felt it was his responsibility to go with the search. He'd actually set out on the first search on May 1, but he had had trouble with his oxygen and had to turn back.

After we'd found Mallory, the obvious goal of a second search was to look for Irvine and the Kodak Vestpocket camera. But by May 15, enough snow had fallen that it seemed unlikely we could find Irvine. Andy and Thom decided instead to go back to Mallory, use a metal detector, and make sure we hadn't missed anything on May 1.

On May 16, the four of us who were headed for the summit climbed up from Camp V to Camp VI. Andy and Thom came up with us, carrying loads to aid our summit push, helped us pitch camp, and then traversed to the west toward Mallory's body.

I'd never met Andy before the expedition, but I knew him

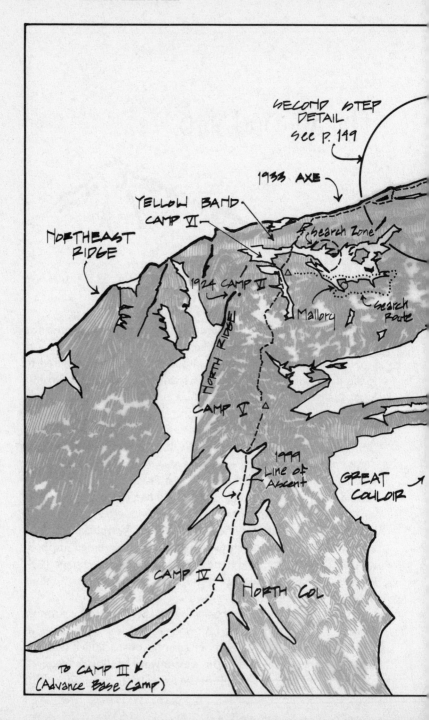

SECOND STEP
DETAIL
see p. 149

1933 AXE

YELLOW BAND
CAMP VI

NORTHEAST
RIDGE

Search Zone

1924 CAMP VI

NORTH RIDGE

Mallory

Search
Route

CAMP V

1999
Line of
Ascent

GREAT
COULOIR

CAMP IV

NORTH COL

TO CAMP III
(Advance Base Camp)

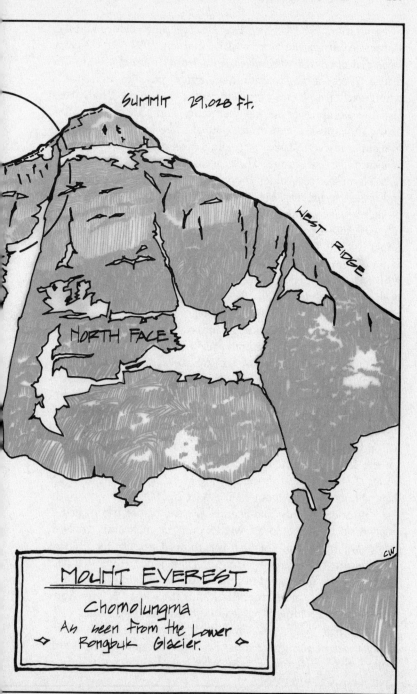

SUMMIT 29,028 ft.

WEST RIDGE

NORTH FACE

MOUNT EVEREST

Chomolungma
As seen from the Lower
Rongbuk Glacier.

by reputation. He'd been to Everest four times before and had summitted from the north with Simo in 1991. He's a very strong climber, thirty-nine years old, from Columbus, Ohio. For fifteen years he was a mountain guide; now he works as a schoolteacher and as a rigger for films and commercials. He's also an accomplished sea kayaker, sailor, and boat builder. Most of the guys on the expedition tended to be long and lean, like me, but Andy's built like a fire plug. He's not tall, and his forearms are like oak stumps. The guy just exudes power.

Thom's a year older than I, at thirty-seven, slender and rather gentle-looking. He's a climber of moderate abilities, and he didn't have as much big-mountain experience as the rest of us, with one expedition to Gasherbrum II in the Karakoram under his belt. On the trail he was really strong. He has a ribald sense of humor—he's a very witty guy. He was a pleasure to be with on this trip, because he would speak his mind; he's honest with other people. Much like Noel Odell in 1924, Thom got stronger as the expedition progressed.

Thom was in an awkward limbo, because he wasn't officially a member of the climbing team, yet he had the same responsibilities as the rest of us. Whenever Simo called for a "mandatory group meeting," the question was, Is Thom expected to attend or not? But he served as a valuable bridge between the climbers and the film crew.

Because they'd carried loads for us from Camp V to Camp VI on the sixteenth, Thom and Andy got a relatively late start on the second search. They didn't branch off to the west until about 2:30 in the afternoon. They were both using oxygen. Later Thom told me about their day at 26,700 feet.

Since only Andy had been to the site before, Thom had to depend on him to relocate Mallory in the makeshift grave of stones we'd piled up. The plan was to head straight for the site, but this turned out to be easier said than done. "Andy just kept walking and walking, not saying anything," Thom told me later. "After a while I said to myself, 'I know he's lost.' Finally Andy said, 'I can't find him.' 'You've gotta be kiddin' me,' I said."

The pair swept back and forth across the ledges where Andy thought the grave must be; with the new snow, everything looked different. Finally, after two hours of wandering, their labor was rewarded.

At the scene, Thom was struck dumb. "It evoked some-thing deeply spiritual," he recalled later. "I kept thinking, this is one of the greatest figures in the history of mountaineering. I got down on my knees and asked for guidance. I prayed, in essence, for guidance not to desecrate the site."

Working silently, the two men removed the stones that covered the body. With the metal detector, Andy found an "arti-fact" our first team had missed. In his pants pocket, Mallory had stuck a wristwatch. The glass was gone from its face, and the minute and second hands were broken off, but the short hour hand pointed to between one and two, a little closer to two. (Later, the hour hand was accidentally broken off as they car-ried the watch down to Base Camp.)

The position of that hand might be a clue to what hap-pened to Mallory and Irvine. Did it imply that the accident had occurred around 1:40? If so, 1:40 P.M., less than an hour after Odell's sighting, or 1:40 A.M., in the middle of a desperate de-scent in the night without a flashlight? Or had the watch stopped working before the accident, and Mallory had stuck it into his pocket? Or had it simply wound down after Mallory's death?

Andy pulled loose a section of the rope to carry down—the rope was so weathered, it broke with a strong tug. And he re-moved the hobnailed boot from Mallory's broken right leg. They brought those objects down, to add to the collection of ar-tifacts.

Thom decided he wanted to look at Mallory's face, which was still frozen into the scree. He cut away the ice and dirt as carefully as he could; as he later put it, "It was like digging into your driveway." At last he got the face freed up enough so that, lying on the ground, he could look straight at George Mallory.

"The face was in perfect condition," Thom said. "It was ever so slightly distorted—pancaked, in effect—by the years of bearing the weight of snow. His eyes were closed. I could still see whiskers on his chin."

As he made his investigation, Thom found the wound that may have caused Mallory's death. "Over his left eye, there was a hole. There was dried blood, and two pieces of skull sticking out. It was as though someone had taken a ball peen hammer and smashed in his forehead."

Finally Andy and Thom reburied the body under the stones. Just as he had the first time, Andy read Psalm 103.

They got back to Camp V late, rappelling the fixed ropes in the dark. As they passed near us at Camp VI, they talked to us on the radio. We wanted to know whether they'd found anything, but once again we were leery of our broadcasts being monitored by other expeditions. Dave Hahn, who knows Morse code, wanted to set up a signal of radio clicks: three clicks followed by two clicks would mean they'd found something. But I thought that could be too hard to remember, especially at altitude, so I came up with another idea.

The code was for me to ask Andy over the radio, "Do you still think I'm an asshole?" The kind of banter climbers trade on the mountain all the time.

Now Andy radioed back, "Yeah, you're still an asshole." That's how we knew they'd found something—but we didn't know what until a couple of days later.

By late afternoon on May 16, we had our tents pitched at Camp VI, just under 27,000 feet. Jake Norton and I shared one tent, Dave Hahn and Tap Richards another, and our two strongest Sherpas, who'd come all the way up from the North Col that day, a third. They were Ang Pasang and Da Nuru, or Dawa for short; among all the Sherpas on our team, they were the two who hoped to go to the top. In addition, Dawa was the sirdar or headman for the expedition. Ang Pasang and Dawa were older and more experienced than most of the other Sherpas, and I thought they had a good chance of summitting. For Sherpas, getting to the top of Everest is important; those who have summitted from both sides are guaranteed steady work. The record for most ascents of Everest—ten—is held by a Sherpa, Ang Rita.

Jake's and my tent faced west. That evening, we watched a magnificent sunset through the door, and fifteen minutes after sunset, in the alpenglow, all the clouds dissipated. We could see Cho Oyu, Pumori, Gyachung Kang, and the Khumbu valley. As the sun set on these lofty sentinels, a warm evening glow enhanced the windless calm. I felt that it was going to be a good day in the morning.

It's difficult to sleep that high. You have all this anticipation and excitement, and you're planning to get up at midnight so you can be off by 2:00 A.M. I'd get about fifteen minutes of random sleep out of each hour. The last hour I lapsed into a deep sleep, and then all of a sudden I had to wake up.

Ang Pasang and Dawa were a little slow getting out of their sleeping bags. We kept hollering over to them to get started. Then my headlamp bulb snapped in the cold, and Dave had to shine his light on my light while I fiddled with the spare bulb in the dark. The headlamp is crucial to moving in the dark and staying warm. As soon as you stop in the predawn cold, you turn into a Popsicle.

With one thing and another, we didn't get off until 2:30 on May 17. In half an hour we reached the foot of the Yellow Band, where the rock changes from gray schistose shale to a tawny limestone. In the dark, it was hard to find the bottom of the fixed ropes that mark the route through the Yellow Band. Only Dave had been there before, and he was able to point out where the fixed lines started.

There were old ropes from previous years on these pitches, but I wasn't about to trust them. I'm very suspicious of fixed lines. Who set the rope and how long ago? What is it anchored to?

We strung out our own fixed rope here, and I was in charge of anchoring it. I felt that it was my responsibility to ensure the safety not only of my teammates, but of the Sherpas. They're paid to be here, and they're putting one hundred percent trust in those lines. If the lines are not secure, you're endangering their lives.

Each of us had a single ascender attached to his harness, which he would slide up the fixed rope as he climbed, sometimes using it to pull on. We were climbing in crampons, even on the rock. It was pretty much pitch dark still; there was a sliver of old moon, but it didn't give much light. Just as dawn started to break, we topped out of the Yellow Band. This is another tricky place, because coming down, when you might be exhausted, you need to find the top of the fixed ropes. Jake and Tap were really heads-up here: anticipating the route-finding problem, they stuck long pickets into the snow, then tied flagging to the heads of the pickets, to make a very visible marker.

At the top of the Yellow Band, we were finally on the

northeast ridge. By now we had turned off our headlamps. The wind was a little brisk, but it wasn't hammering us. A lenticular cloud was forming on the summit, which is usually not a good sign. We tucked ourselves into the shelter of a boulder and had our first discussion.

Tap and Jake are both twenty-five, more than a decade younger than Dave and I. I often shared a tent with Jake; we really hit it off, I think because our paces and cycles were very similar. I'd first met him in Kathmandu in 1996, when we happened to stay in the same hotel. It was good to see him again on this expedition.

Jake has done some guiding, but he makes a living refurbishing old houses and renting out units in Colorado Springs, where he lives. He'd spent considerable time in Kathmandu, studying Buddhism, and had learned to speak Nepali. So our views and values were remarkably compatible.

Jake's a genuinely nice and honest person. He never got upset about anything. On our expedition, I thought of Jake as the strongest member. Whenever we had to build camp sites, he'd carry a huge number of rocks. On the long trek to ABC, Jake would keep pace with the Sherpas, chatting away in Nepali. He's about six feet one or two, 170 pounds, a big, lanky guy, about the same size and height as me.

Tap's an inch or two shorter, and even leaner than I—also a lanky fellow. He too was very strong. He'd been on several Himalayan expeditions and was sensitive to the nuances of getting along with teammates in an inhospitable place. Tap lives in Taos, New Mexico, but cut his teeth on Rainier and now guides for IMG, Simo's company. Among the mountains he guides are Denali and Aconcagua. Also a very likable guy. At Base Camp, during rest days, Tap and I came together around a certain ritual of what we called "carbo loading" and washing our socks. It's important to have clean socks on a big Himalayan mountain, because your feet stay dryer. Tap and I would build a little wash basin behind the storage tent, sneak a few beers out there, and drink them with the Sherpas on the sly while we did our laundry.

The interesting thing, in view of subsequent events, was that shortly after dawn, as we huddled behind the Conference Rock (as I called it) on the northeast ridge, at about 27,700 feet, it was Dave Hahn who felt the least confident. He was the first to express his doubts about going on. "Hey, man, I'm really cold," he said. "This doesn't look like a good day. That lenticular isn't good. I think the weather's going to turn bad on us. We need to make a decision right here."

Jake and Tap seemed caught up in a certain lassitude and indecisiveness. They weren't totally jazzed to go on. They may have been a bit intimidated. For that matter, we were all intimidated, way up there on the northeast ridge. We knew that the obstacles ahead, the First and Second Steps and the traverse between them, were very serious ground. Ang Pasang and Dawa hardly said a word. I felt that we ought to keep going and see how the day turned out. I knew we could at least get to the base of the First Step, some 250 yards away. I wanted to keep going—I was getting cold just sitting there, swinging my feet and arms to try to stay warm—and then the Sherpas said, "Yes, let's go."

We must have spent forty-five minutes at Conference Rock in this discussion. We talked on the radio to Simo down at ABC, to get his input on the weather. We were all breathing oxygen, at a flow of two and a half to three and a half liters per minute. I'd originally hoped to climb Everest without oxygen, but after seeing what had happened to the Ukrainians, I opted for gas as giving us an added safety margin.

It was very near here that Percy Wyn Harris found the ice axe that belonged to either Mallory or Irvine, in 1933. And slightly to the west of this spot, on their way down later that day, Tap and Jake found an old oxygen bottle and carried it down the mountain. Back at Base Camp, Jochen Hemmleb was able to determine that it was definitely a 1924 bottle. Simo had actually seen the bottle in 1991; now he was kicking himself for not having retrieved it then. The bottle is another vital piece of evidence, for it further proves that Mallory and Irvine at least reached a point just short of the First Step, and that they were on the skyline ridge, not traversing the face below.

So we started on. Dave was the official leader of the party; but since I was breaking trail and stringing the fixed ropes, I became the de facto leader. At the foot of the First Step, I was going first, with the two Sherpas right behind. I had to fix another rope on the Step, but to climb it I clipped in to the old fixed ropes. What I did was to put more than my weight on those old lines by bouncing up and down on them while I was still in a secure place. That way I was testing them with more impact than they would bear if I fell going up. The Sherpas payed out the new rope as I led the Step, sliding my ascender up the old fixed ropes. At the top, I anchored the new line by tying it to long, thin pitons that other parties had driven into the rock. This was not only time-consuming; I also had to take off my mittens and wear only fleece gloves while I tied the knots.

The First Step was very exposed fourth-class climbing; if it had been any harder, we would have roped up and belayed. Mallory could have done it. I doubt that he and Irvine would have gone where the ropes go today; more likely they would have climbed the Step on the left hand side of the ridge, closer to the Kangshung Face. This may be the place where they were when Noel Odell caught his famous glimpse of them outlined against the sky.

Above the First Step, I started the traverse to the Second. This is very tricky ground; there are dangerous pockets of deep snow, and the whole traverse is underlain with downsloping, loose, shaley stones. The route goes a little below the crest of the ridge, over the north face. I didn't string out new rope here; that would have taken too long, and besides, we had no rope to spare. In place there was a single strand of thin old rope, maybe six millimeters in diameter, severely abraded in places. As I moved along, I took up the slack in the fixed line and tied it off at intervals to make it safer.

Forty-five minutes along the traverse, halfway to the Second Step, I came to a feature that's called the Mushroom Rock. It's a mushroom-shaped bollard of rock maybe seven feet tall. I went around to the east side of it, out of the wind, in the sun, and for the first time that day, I got warm.

Amazingly enough, in 1975 the Chinese team put their Camp VII here, the highest camp ever pitched on Everest. They installed twenty climbers here. (There were some 400 members of the expedition!)

At the Mushroom Rock, we regrouped for the second time. Dave switched his oxygen cylinder. We knew he was going on a higher flow than the rest of us, maybe four liters per minute, because he thought he would need the extra gas to shoot video all the way, which was his role. Later that increased flow would have consequences.

The traverse from the First Step to the Mushroom Rock proved to be very demanding, with insecure footing and the weather changing constantly. After a while, Tap and Jake came up. I could see that the look in their eyes had changed.

Weeks before, down at Base Camp, we'd had long discussions about this sort of moment. I always said to the others, You can't go for the summit because you feel obligated to. You can't do it because you want to shoot pictures. You can't do it because you want to write a story about it. And you can't do it for someone else, because that someone else won't be there if you screw up. You have to do it because you're really motivated from inside, because you have your own personal reasons to do it.

I've had partners get wishy-washy on other big climbs, and I've said to them, "Let's go down." If they are not into it, we're going to get in trouble. At Base Camp, when Tap and Jake heard my views, one of them said, "Wow, that sounds pretty harsh."

Now they said, "Hey, it's just not in the cards. I can't see us going on. The weather's not looking good." They had decided to turn around.

Part of their reasoning may have had to do with their training as guides. When you guide, your assessment of risk has to be conservative. If, when they were eighteen, they'd gone after climbing hard and had the drive to make really difficult first ascents, instead of starting out as guides, perhaps now at twenty-five they would have wanted to go on.

I said, "Hey, the decision is one hundred percent yours. I'm going to go on. I feel comfortable with what I see up here. But I understand how you feel, and I appreciate your judgment." We got on the radio again and told Simo that Jake and Tap were turning around. He didn't have any trouble with that. The main thing in his mind was that some of us were going to push on for the summit.

Later Tap amplified his feelings at that moment. "Things just didn't feel right. We'd seen what happened to the Ukrainians. There was a bit of a feeling that death was breathing in our faces."

"It was the hardest decision I've ever made in the mountains," Jake added. "I was in tears."

For me, the weather, far from seeming ominous, had just improved. The lenticular was gone from the summit. I was warmer than I'd been all day. And Dave's mood had completely turned around. He was in great spirits, totally psyched. He and I were clicking. He seemed now to be picking up on my vibe.

Dave was the person who'd gotten me invited to Mount Everest. He and I had climbed together before, during two seasons in Antarctica. Dave is the chief guide for Adventure Network International down there, guiding Mount Vinson, which he's climbed fourteen times, the record. Dave and I did the classic route on Mount Gardner, and we climbed an unnamed 5,000-foot pyramid nearby. Last winter, we discovered two caches left by the first American team to climb Gardner, in 1967. As we ate thirty-two-year-old chocolate, Dave and I joked about the upcoming Everest expedition.

Dave's thirty-seven years old, tall and craggy-looking. He's a really solid big-mountain guide. Very good with clients—patient and understanding. He's got a wry sense of humor, with a weakness for puns. I think he'd like to be a professional writer: he put a tremendous amount of effort into his Internet dispatches, which were the cream of the Mountain-Zone reportage. He's also serious about becoming a filmmaker. On summit day, he was determined to shoot video for *NOVA* all the way to the top.

This was Dave's fourth expedition to Everest. In 1994 he had summitted, but the climb turned into an epic. This was also an expedition led by Simo. On May 19 of that year, Dave set out for the top with an Italian climber, who turned back at the Second Step. Dave went on alone, summitting at 4:45 P.M., which is pretty late, but he'd made the first successful ascent of the season. He had to do most of the descent in the dark, and he was forced to bivouac just above the First Step. Breathing oxygen during the night, he miraculously avoided frostbite. Just before dawn, a teammate came out to meet him with food, water, and extra oxygen. He found Dave dehydrated and exhausted, yet they managed to get back to camp safely.

A week later, tragedy struck the north side of Everest. An Australian, Michael Rheinberger, set out for the top with the

New Zealander Mark Whetu. Rheinberger was fifty-three years old and had tried Everest seven times before without making it; this time he was determined to summit. He and Whetu finally summitted at 7:18 P.M. They had to bivouac in the open just twenty yards below the summit. Amazingly, they survived the night, but the next day, after eleven hours of all-out effort, they'd only gotten down to the Second Step. By now Rheinberger was blind, delirious, and unable to walk. The winds were so strong that potential rescuers sent up from Camp VI had to turn back at the First Step. Finally Whetu had to abandon his friend just to save his own life. It was a close call even so, and he suffered severe frostbite. Rheinberger got his summit, but it cost him his life.

There might be those who would criticize Dave Hahn for pushing on in '94 and reaching the summit so late. Dave knows the value of turning back when he needs to. On his other two previous Everest expeditions, he turned around both times at 28,000 feet.

After deciding to go down, Tap and Jake waited for a while at the Mushroom Rock to watch us try to climb the Second Step. As I headed off again, I assumed the Sherpas were coming. But at that moment, Ang Pasang decided to drop out too. He stayed with Tap and Jake and then descended with them. He didn't tell me he was turning back, so I didn't even get a chance to say goodbye to him.

The continuation of the traverse, between the Mushroom Rock and the Second Step, is at least as tricky as the first half. The loose rock alternates with deep pockets where the snow ranges from knee- to even waist-deep. On some of those pockets, there was no fixed rope in place. They were quite spooky. You had to be alert: if the snow started sliding, it could take you off the hill and send you flying down to the Rongbuk. As I led this traverse, I thought often about Mallory and Irvine crossing the same terrain in 1924.

I got to the base of the Second Step and waited for Dave and Dawa. I was feeling strong enough that day that even breaking trail, I'd get ten, fifteen, twenty, or more minutes ahead of the others. Now Dawa came up, sort of shaking his head. I looked at him, and he said, "I'm going to go down." I said, "I understand. No problem." He gave me the last fixed rope, which I cached there to use on the descent. I wasn't worried about Dawa traversing back to the First Step by himself. The experienced Sherpas are very surefooted on that sort of terrain. I knew he'd catch up to Jake, Tap, and Ang Pasang before too long.

So it was down to Dave and me. We turned to face the Second Step. It was about 10:30 in the morning. We weren't going super-fast, but the pace seemed all right, and the weather looked good.

THE SECOND STEP is an unlikely barrier, ninety feet high, on what would otherwise be a moderate ridge. The bottom section is angular and blocky; the best route up it surmounts a series of high steps and mantles. In the middle of the Step, a snow triangle leans against the cliff. Above that, a fifteen-foot crack in a large corner, slightly overhanging, forms the crux of the climb. It was here that the Chinese in 1975 affixed their ladder. Ten feet of less steep rock above the ladder complete the cliff.

As Dave joined me at the bottom of the Second Step, which was in shade, he said, "Darn it, the video camera's fogging up." We'd have to pop open the cassette and dry it out in the sun, so I suggested he ascend the fixed ropes to the base of the ladder, where he could get back into the sunlight, then work on the camera.

Dave jugged up the rope, got to the top of the snow triangle, and clipped in to the base of the ladder. Then I rock-climbed the first forty-five feet, using my ascender on the fixed rope to catch me should I slip. The climbing was moderately hard, but not extreme. By the time I got up to the ladder, Dave got the camera working intermittently.

At this point I took off my pack with the oxygen apparatus. I'd decided to try the free-climb without oxygen, mainly because the rig was so cumbersome, the mask protruding so that I couldn't properly see my feet with it on. I pulled a 112-foot-long line out of my pack, a good climbing rope nine millimeters in diameter, and tied in to the rope. Dave would belay me with that. He wanted to shoot video while belaying, but I needed a good, secure belay here, and the video would have to take second priority. You can't both shoot well and belay safely.

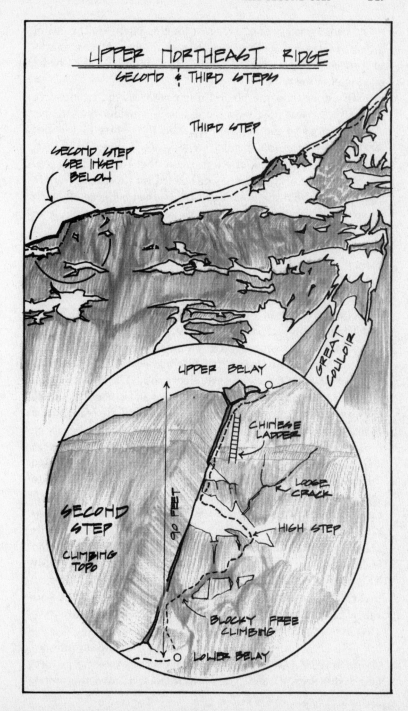

UPPER NORTHEAST RIDGE
SECOND & THIRD STEPS

THIRD STEP

SECOND STEP
SEE INSET
BELOW

GREAT COULOIR

UPPER BELAY

CHINESE LADDER

LOOSE CRACK

HIGH STEP

SECOND STEP

CLIMBING TOPO

90 FEET

BLOCKY FREE CLIMBING

LOWER BELAY

I had a small rack of gear just for this pitch—four cams of different sizes and six Stoppers, devices climbers place in cracks to shorten a potential fall. I got my rack organized, then had a good look at the crux.

To understand the pivotal importance of the twenty-five feet of rock I was now facing, one has to consider the strange, murky history of the Second Step. The 1924 party had looked hard at that bump on the skyline from far below. On June 4, Teddy Norton had traversed through the Yellow Band well below the crest of the ridge, as he headed for the Great Couloir, explicitly to avoid the Step. But Mallory had believed all along in an attack on the crest of the ridge—that was his style of climbing. And in his famous sighting, Noel Odell had initially believed that it was the Second Step he saw the two tiny figures surmount in only five minutes.

With the closure of the north side of Everest to foreigners after 1938, no one again came anywhere near the Second Step until 1960. That year, a huge Chinese expedition—214 Chinese and Tibetan climbers, none of whom, however, had more than five years' experience in the mountains—assaulted Everest from the north. The stories that filtered back to the West from this mass assault puzzled nearly everybody. The main account available in English appeared in a propaganda magazine called *China Reconstructs*. It reads more like a homiletic Maoist tract than a mountaineering narrative. According to that article, an initial pair of would-be summiteers flailed away at the Step for a long afternoon and into the night, climbing all but the last "three meters," before enduring a grim bivouac in a crevice, then descending the next day. Three weeks later, another trio came to grips with the Step. One man made four all-out attempts to solve the crux, falling off exhausted each time. Finally another climber, Chu Yin-hua, took off his gloves and boots, used a shoulder stand, and had a go at the cliff in stocking feet. The partner who hoisted him up "trembled all over, short of breath, but he clenched his teeth and steadily stood up, with much heroic effort." Topping the cliff after a three-hour struggle, Chu brought his comrades up on a tight rope.

Three men then supposedly continued to the summit, arriving at 4:20 A.M. Because it was dark, they took no pictures above the Second Step. The summitteers claimed they left a plaster bust of Mao on top, but it has never been found. For his heroic effort, Chu later lost his fingers and feet to frostbite.

A lot of Western climbers felt then, and many still feel that this Chinese ascent was a hoax. After summarizing the *China Reconstructs* account in the *American Alpine Journal,* editor H. Adams Carter, who was an absolute stickler for accuracy, dryly editorialized, "The details are such that mountaineers in nearly all parts of the climbing world have received the news with considerable skepticism."

The next alleged ascent of the north ridge, also by Chinese, came in 1975, during the expedition on which Wang Hongbao found his "old English dead." From their comrades in 1960, these climbers learned all about the difficulty of the Second Step. Having ferried all kinds of gear up to their Camp VII at the Mushroom Rock, the team hauled their ladder up to the crux, tied it to pitons they pounded into cracks in the rock, then climbed the ladder. All subsequent ascents of the north ridge have used the ladder and/or the fixed ropes now strung in place on the Step.

Mallory and Irvine, of course, had had no ladder. This was why I wanted to free-climb the Second Step, for unless Mallory and Irvine made it, the crux had never been free-climbed. (Even the 1960 shoulder stand, if not a piece of fiction, has to be classified as artificial climbing.)

In recent years, several climbers who used the ladder wondered whether another crack about ten feet to the right might serve as a possible route. Before I tackled the wall beside the ladder, I sidled out to the right to check out this alternative. I couldn't start from the top of the snow triangle, but had to kick steps down the edge of it to get to the crack. The rock was so rotten, none of my cams or Stoppers would have held. If I had come off on this crack, I would have taken a very bad fall. Finally I got to the base of the crack. It was filled with loose, disjointed rock, really dangerous. I just stood there, picking up grapefruit-sized stones in my hands and moving them around. The crack just wasn't an option.

This illustrated for me the limitations of all the theoretical approaches to the Mallory and Irvine mystery that have been advanced over the years. Jochen Hemmleb had become fascinated with the Second Step. In previous years, he'd written three lengthy "research papers" about it, posting them on the Internet. One was called "How to Get Up the Second Step—A Topo Guide." In his latest paper, Hemmleb had gone so far as to rate the crack I was now investigating. "If free-climbed," he postulated, "the original headwall pitch is probably Grade IV–V (British 4b, USA 5.6)." All this, without his ever having seen Mount Everest! Even on this expedition, Jochen never got higher than a little above the North Col, at 23,000 feet. None of this kept him from being the world's leading expert on features like the Second Step. In the lower camps, I'd hear him say, "There are many climbers on this expedition, but I am irreplaceable."

I decided that the only place to climb the Step was right where the ladder had been tied in. I started to the left of the ladder, where a crack angles up and right. I left my crampons on, because it would have been too much effort to take them off, and I knew it might be icy at the top of the pitch. Besides, I felt comfortable climbing hard rock with crampons on.

The exposure here was unbelievable—8,000 feet of space down to the Rongbuk Glacier. I knew I was going to have to move fast, because that's the way to go on hard routes, especially at an altitude as high as 28,230 feet. If you rest and hang on to a hold too long, you just flame out. I started up with an arm bar and a knee jam; then I stepped onto some tiny edges with my right foot. Dave had hoped to film my lead, but as soon as I started climbing, it was all he could do to stay alert and pay out the rope. It was in his interest to pay attention, because once I got above him, if I'd popped off and landed on him with my crampons, we could both have been badly injured.

It wasn't until I got about fifteen feet above Dave that I could place my first and only piece of protection. There was a chockstone wedged in the crack, underneath which I placed a perfect hand-sized cam. As soon as I clipped my rope to the cam, I felt better. At this point, I had to step right. Now I had a hand jam with my left hand, my right hand on a sloping hold, my left foot jammed in the crack, and I was only about six inches away from the ladder. The place I needed to put my right foot was between the rungs of the ladder. It was really awkward—the ladder was in the way.

I reached my foot between the rungs, but at that point I

was panting, totally winded. I just had to step on the rung and rest.

I rested just long enough to unleash a string of swear words and catch my breath. I was mad because by stepping on the rung, I'd compromised my free climb. Then I moved on up. There was one tricky move, and then the cliff sloped back. I led on up to the anchor, which is a coffee-table-sized boulder sitting on a ledge, backed up with several knife-blade pitons pounded into some shallow, fissurelike cracks. All the fixed ropes are tied to this anchor.

I tied in, gave myself some slack, crept back to the edge of the cliff, and had Dave tie in my pack so I could haul it up. Then Dave climbed the ladder, ascending the fixed ropes.

I hadn't free-climbed the Second Step. That achievement still awaits a stronger climber. I had done all but one move, yet I'd failed in what I set out to do. Nonetheless, the effort had given me a good idea of how hard the climb was. At the time, erring on the side of caution, I tentatively graded the pitch at 5.8. Later, when I got back to the States and saw at what level I was climbing in Yosemite and Indian Creek, Utah, I changed my mind. The Second Step is probably a solid 5.10. And that's a lot harder than anything climbers were doing in Wales, with plimsoll shoes, hemp ropes, no pitons, and a "gentleman's belay" (with no anchor to the rock), in the early 1920s.

I got on the radio to Simo. I said right off the bat that I hadn't free-climbed the Step. I told him I'd been weak, I'd had to step on the ladder at one point.

I'd done the twenty-five feet quickly, in about five minutes. It was 11:00 A.M. now. We left the climbing rack there, an empty water bottle, a couple of other odds and ends. Before we started on, I asked Dave, "How are you feeling? Are you psyched to go on?" I felt it was important to present him with the option. I said, "Dave, if you want to go down, I understand. I can get to the top from here on my own. I feel comfortable on this terrain."

Right away he answered, "Let's go for the summit."

ABOVE THE SECOND STEP, the ridge broadens into a region called the Plateau. The going here is relatively easy; there are only a couple of little rock towers you have to climb over. I was actually getting warm here, so I unzipped the sides of my down suit to ventilate. On the Plateau, we passed near the bodies of two Indian climbers who had died here in 1996, the year of all the deaths chronicled in *Into Thin Air*. These were the Indians whom members of the Japanese team had ignored, going for the summit themselves rather than trying to save their lives. We went within about thirty yards of them, but I didn't look at them up close.

We climbed the Third Step, an enjoyable scramble, much easier than the First or Second. At the top of that, we were at the base of the summit pyramid, only some 500 feet below the top of the mountain. I was so warm I started to take off the top of my down jacket, but all of a sudden a snow squall hit. It began snowing thick, heavy, wet flakes.

I started traversing up and right across the summit pyramid. The snow underfoot got deeper and deeper, until it was mid-thigh. I'd gotten a bit ahead of Dave here. With my ski stick, I could probe down through the loose snow and hit a hard layer of ice beneath. The slope was about 45 degrees. I kept crossing small, bell-shaped pockets of windslab snow that were particularly likely to avalanche. I started to get really concerned.

I radioed down, "Dave, this is not good. Do you mind waiting there? We've got to load this slope one person at a time." I went ahead while Dave waited. My intuition, from years of being in the mountains and studying snow pack and snow texture, told me this was really dangerous.

I got on the radio again, to talk to Simo and Russell Brice at ABC. At one point, Simo said, "You guys just get on up there and ring the bell and get on down." He was understandably invested in someone from our expedition making the summit. I didn't feel manipulated, but his words were a bit too gung ho. I kept worrying: This is not safe. Then I'd reflect that the Ukrainians had crossed here without incident; but that was nine days earlier, and the conditions could have been entirely different.

Russell Brice got on the radio. He's climbed Everest from the north three times. In a droll voice, he said, "The summit pyramid's always like that. It's always a bit spooky. I've had to traverse it the way you are each time I've been up there." That was valuable advice for me; that was real information I could use.

I could see rock ahead, the ridgeline where I knew there'd be hard snow, thanks to its being exposed to the wind. I didn't come close to turning around here, but it was the one time on the expedition I really had to stick my neck out. I figured, I've just got to punch through and hope my karma is good.

By 1:30, I had reached the rock at the top of the traverse. I sat down to wait for Dave. Then I realized that I was at the exact spot where Rheinberger and Whetu had made their desperate bivouac in 1994. I was only sixty feet below the summit.

I waited there for forty minutes, on the lee side of the slope, out of the wind. I took my oxygen set off, sat on a rock bench, and tried to dry out my glove liners and fleece hat.

Simo kept coming on the radio, saying, "What's up?"

I said, "I'm having a great time here, just enjoying the view."

"Where's Dave?"

"He's fine. He's coming up."

Each time Simo talked to me, he sounded more anxious. "All right, good job. We're totally psyched and really hoping you guys can get up there."

I had to say, "I'm going to wait for Dave before I go to the summit." It was a team thing. If it weren't for Dave, I wouldn't have been on the expedition.

At last Dave came into sight. I could see that he was breathing hard, looking out of it. Then suddenly, just as he got up to me, he was ill.

On Himalayan expeditions, everyone is exposed to strains of unfamiliar bacteria. Your intestinal tract is constantly assaulted. Now Dave was struck with a sudden wave of nausea and diarrhea. He almost got his suit open in time. So right there, sixty feet below the summit, he had to open up his trousers, clean himself up, and seal his suit back up. Maybe it was just a stomach bug, but when you're severely stressed, one of the first parts of your system to react is your digestive tract. What had happened to Dave was no reflection on his toughness, nor was it personally humiliating. It simply proved that Everest is always a serious mountain if someone as strong as he could be reduced to the thinnest of margins.

In the Karakoram once, I was struck by a similar violent incontinence midway through a dangerous icefall. To this date, it stands as one of my most unpleasant experiences in climbing. I could empathize with Dave, yet what alarmed me was not so much the diarrhea as the nausea and the depleted look on his face.

"Dave, do we need to turn around?" I asked.

He said, "No, no, let's go to the top." But his words were very slow. I was thinking, This is really bad. Dave's not in good shape.

People get too blasé about Everest, especially people who've never been there. All the talk about it being a routine climb, a walk-up. Even experienced veterans can fall into that thinking, like Scott Fischer with his "yellow brick road" in 1996.

I gave Dave some of my warm energy drink. Then I said, "You go ahead and take the final steps to the summit first. I wouldn't be here without you."

He got about halfway there, then stopped. "Something is wrong," he said in a hoarse voice. "Check my oxygen."

I checked his bottle and saw that it was on zero. With a four-liter flow, he'd used up his second bottle. I took the empty bottle off and pitched it down the Kangshung Face. Usually I'm adamant about bringing all the oxygen cylinders down and having them refilled. In our predicament, however, neither Dave nor I could afford to lug those fourteen pounds of dead weight. I justified tossing the bottle as less of an eyesore than leaving it beside the track to the summit.

Dave put his pack back on, and we climbed up to the summit without oxygen. It was 2:50 P.M., later than we would have liked. We spent only about ten minutes on top. Dave filmed the last few steps to the top, though the lens was really fogged, and we took a few pictures of each other. I got out the walnut from the *puja* at Bouddanath and left it there. And I had a film canister filled with rice from the monks at the Rongbuk Monastery; I threw the rice over my left shoulder onto the summit. We were surrounded by clouds. There was nothing to see beyond the small cone of snow—a humble apex to the highest mountain on earth.

I had always dreamed of this moment as a supreme experience. Today, it was not. I stood on top of the world, yet I felt scared and overwhelmed.

It had stopped snowing. I looked at my watch and thought, It's three o'clock. We've only got four hours before dark. My partner is not doing very well. We're in a serious predicament.

The terrain below, which we'd have to down-climb, amounted to a very serious route. It's not like on the south side below the south summit, where for long stretches you can sit on your rear end and slide. If Dave were to collapse, there was no way I could lower him down the route. If I had then stayed with him, we might both have perished.

When we got back to the Rheinberger-Whetu bivouac site, I took the oxygen cylinder out of my pack and gave it to Dave, turned to a flow of two liters per minute. Then I took all the stuff he'd been carrying and put it in my pack. I gave him more fluid, and I said, "Dave, we've got to really work together on this. We've got to do it well."

He seemed disconnected from reality, and I was very concerned, because I'd never seen him like that before, even on our hardest days together in Antarctica. "How do you want to descend?" I asked. "Do you want me to go first, or do you want to go first?" He asked me to lead, which was good, because it would be easier for him to follow in my footsteps.

We climbed back down the dangerous traverse. Dave was very slow. Every place where there was a little bit of rock, I'd wait till he caught up, then when he did, I'd start off right away. This may have been a mistake: maybe I should have given him a chance to rest. But by now, I realized that at this pace we were likely to face an open bivouac.

At the top of the Third Step, I set up a rappel. I rigged Dave's rappel device for him, so that all he had to do was clip it in to the rope. But when he came down, I saw that he'd just wrapped the rope around his arms; he hadn't used the rappel device at all. When I pointed this out to him, he said, "I'm fine. Leave me alone."

"No, you're not," I said. "Dave, this is a really serious situation. We need to team together and do this right. The rig I set up for you is going to help you out." If he'd clipped in with his rappel device, even if he lost control and started to fall, I could stop him by pulling the bottom of the rappel rope tight. Since he'd only wrapped the rope around his arms, if he'd fallen, he might have gone flying right off the mountain.

I was moving all right without oxygen. I hadn't planned to use it on the descent, because I wanted to see my feet as clearly as possible. Below the Third Step, we started across the Plateau. It was about 4:00 P.M. Now Dave got even slower. He was really out of it, stopping and sitting down. He was deteriorating even further. I kept calculating our pace, the amount of oxygen Dave had, and the hours of daylight we had left. At all costs I wanted to avoid a bivouac. A night out with neither tent nor stove at the least would have meant frostbite, at the worst, death. It seemed vital to get to the base of the First Step before dark.

A little before 5:00 P.M., I made a very hard decision. The Ukrainians had come to grief on May 8 in part because they had waited till 9:00 P.M. before radioing for help. So I got on the radio to Simo. "Is it possible," I asked, "next time you speak to Tap and Jake at Camp VI, you can ask them to grab some hot drinks, some oxygen, and some headlamp batteries and start cruising up the Yellow Band and meet us somewhere?"

Simo was great about this. At once he said, "Good idea. We need to do it." He radioed Tap and Jake. By then, Ang Pasang and Dawa had already headed on down the mountain, planning to go all the way to ABC that night. I knew how hard it would be for Tap and Jake to head up again, just when they'd reached camp and settled into it. I was worried that at some point I'd run out of the energy it was taking to keep Dave going, and I'd have a hard time taking care of myself.

At the top of the Second Step, I tied the good 112-foot rope to the anchor, so that we could rappel down it. This time I made sure Dave was okay, that he was going to clip in with his rappel device after I had unclipped at the bottom. As I went down first on rappel, I had to pay the rope out ahead of me. At the bottom I tied off the end of the rope, then hollered, "Off rappel!" Dave was out of sight on the shelf above. So I repeated the call over the radio.

I began the task of stringing out the fixed rope that Dawa had carried up to here. Between the Second Step and the Mushroom Rock, there was a bad stretch I wanted to fix. The rope was pretty tangled, so I had to focus. I didn't see Dave coming down yet, which worried me further, but then the rope on the Second Step started jiggling, and I knew he was on rappel.

We got to the Mushroom Rock at 6:30, just as the sun was setting. I put on another layer of long underwear uppers. I was still in fairly good shape myself. Over the years, I've learned that I can go strong for about eighteen hours, which we were now approaching. After this I get a second wind and I can go another eight hours. If I stay out past twenty-six hours, my chance of returning unharmed is diminished. After forty-eight hours in these conditions, I would be totally cooked.

Dave caught up with me at the Mushroom Rock. He'd left his first oxygen bottle here, with a thousand pounds of pressure still in it. We switched his cylinders over and headed down.

Later, down at Base Camp, Simo was upset with Dave. He chewed him out for cranking his oxygen flow so high and running out of gas on the summit. It caused a lot of tension, and it took a few days for them to work it out. I just tried to stay out of the whole business. I didn't think Dave had gotten in over his head, since we'd climbed together before. Eventually he and Simo were reconciled.

But the other thing they discussed was how to present what happened on summit day to the world. Eric said that we had to agree on an official account that would be what the public would hear, and that it would be a challenge for us to do this in a way that reflected positively on everyone involved. I think he felt that a near-fiasco might undermine the story of the successful search expedition he had led.

But Dave said, "If we don't tell the whole truth, Conrad doesn't get the credit he deserves."

I said, "It just doesn't matter."

Now, at the Mushroom Rock, the fresh oxygen bottle rejuvenated Dave. He started coming back. With the ropes fixed below, we moved pretty well. We got off rappel at the foot of the First Step just at dusk. Now we were on easy terrain. Rather than take a break to put on our headlamps, I said, "Dave, let's go, let's really make time."

For the first time, as Dave started getting his energy back, I stopped being so worried. Things were going to be okay. I knew that Jake and Tap were on their way up, because by now we were talking to them on the radio. The one tricky place left was the top of the Yellow Band—you're tempted to cut down too soon, but you need to find the top of the fixed ropes that take you through the Band. I got a little off route here, which led to a macabre moment. I came around a cliff and looked into a small cave right next to me. There was a dead man lying in there— somebody who'd holed up there trying to bivouac and had frozen to death. I have no idea who he was.

With this victim fresh in mind, I asked Dave, You've been here three times before—can you find the exit cracks at the top of the Yellow Band? He located the pickets that marked the top of the fixed ropes.

Tap and Jake met us midway through the Yellow Band. They had a fresh oxygen bottle, hot drinks in a Thermos, and some food, though nobody wanted to eat. We just sat there, chatting quietly, with every now and then an outburst of enthusiasm. It was a good little meeting.

I got down to Camp VI by 9:15, the other three twenty minutes later. Once we were in our sleeping bags, Dave leaned on one elbow and said wearily, "Man, thanks for looking after me."

But the experience didn't really hit home till late the next day. In the morning, Dave and I slept in, feebly brewing pots of hot water, before climbing on down to ABC. On the snow field below Camp VI, we crossed paths with climbers from other expeditions heading up; they greeted us with big smiles and hearty congratulations.

At the moment when we got off the last fixed line at the base of the North Col, with all the dangers behind us, in the middle of a snow flurry, Dave and I turned to each other and embraced. We'd made it.

Apotheosis

WHEN WE GOT DOWN TO ABC, the whole team, film crew and Sherpas and climbers, had a big celebration. Sherpa Pemba had baked us a two-layer cake. I was happy and proud of what we had done, not so much because we'd summitted as because we'd come off the mountain with no frostbite, no serious injuries, no fatalities.

Yet the celebration was muted by what was going on higher on the mountain at that very moment. As we'd descended, two other expeditions—a Polish one and a Belgian one—were headed up for their own summit attempts. On the afternoon of May 18, the day after Dave and I summitted, three climbers from the Polish team and two from the Belgian got to the top.

We'd seen them on the afternoon of the eighteenth along the summit ridge. They were going at a good pace, and then it was as though they suddenly hit a patch of glue. The exertion they'd already made took its toll: they were slowed almost to a crawl. On the way down, apparently, they got strung out and separated.

The same thing happened to the Poles and Belgians that had happened to the Ukrainians on May 8. Only one member of each party got back to Camp VI the night of the eighteenth. Two Poles and a Belgian had to bivouac.

One of the Poles, Tadusz Kudelski, may have slipped and fallen off the ridge somewhere between the First and Second

Steps; he was never seen again. The other Pole who spent the night out was Ryszard Pawlowski, a very strong climber who'd summitted before on Everest. He made it back to Camp VI on May 19, but with serious frostbite. His ordeal proved once more just how formidable Everest is.

Even the Belgian team member who made it back to camp on the eighteenth—actually a Portuguese climber named João Garcia—got frostbite on the nose, soles of feet, and hands. The other Belgian was their expedition leader, the well-known veteran Pascal Debrouwer. Some Sherpas went up to try to rescue him and found him near the base of the First Step. They couldn't rouse him: he was essentially comatose, so they had to return empty-handed. And then—this is speculation—I think the warmth of the afternoon sun must have brought Debrouwer around, because he got up, took a few shaky steps, lost control, and fell off the ridge. We know this because some climbers at Camp VI witnessed his fall.

On the nineteenth, we descended all the way to Base Camp. That evening we had another celebration—with a gallon of Scotch shared among the climbers and Sherpas; we got hammered, and everybody danced, including the Sherpas. But before I walked into our camp to start celebrating, I stopped at the Belgian tent. I found two team members there, really stricken. It was Debrouwer's third try for the summit; and on this attempt he left behind a wife and children. His fate was a powerful reminder of the wrath of Everest. His teammates were starting to figure out how to contact his family. I offered them the use of our satellite phone, then spent half an hour trying to console them.

By now, the news of our discovery of Mallory had caused a sensation all over the world. The MountainZone Web site averaged a million hits a day for two weeks. The publication of photos of Mallory's body in *Newsweek*, *Stern*, and the English and Australian tabloids had cranked up the controversy a notch. We were still worried about whether the Chinese might impede our return from the mountain with arcane customs hassles, or even confiscate the artifacts.

In the end, our fears proved groundless, as various team members carried Mallory's belongings in their baggage back to the States, where Simo put them under the curatorial care of

the Washington State Historical Museum in Tacoma. Ultimately, both the Mallory family and the expedition members
would like to see these objects form a permanent museum exhi-
bition. The letters have been donated to Magdalene College,
Cambridge, where they will be archived with the rich correspondence between Ruth and George.

ALL THE WAY to the mountain in March, we'd discussed whether
Mallory or Irvine could have made the summit. Jochen Hemmleb was a walking encyclopedia of lore about all three expeditions in the 1920s, but he got so obsessive about the minutiae
that sometimes he couldn't see the forest for the trees. By the
time we started up the mountain in April, I'd have to say that
most of us were dubious about the possibility the two lost
climbers had made the top.

Finding Mallory, however, had a galvanic effect upon my
teammates' judgment. After the expedition, Hemmleb said, "I
give them a sixty-forty or a fifty-fifty chance they made the
summit." Tap Richards leaned further in their favor: "I think
they made it. Odds are tough to calculate, but I'd say maybe
seventy-thirty." And Jake Norton was completely turned
around. "Seeing George Mallory changed my mind," he said.
"He was awe-inspiring in death. Maybe it's idealism on my
part, maybe I just want to believe, but I'd say the odds are
ninety-ten he made the summit."

I'm sorry to say that I can't agree with these sanguine opin-
ions. I'd be as thrilled as anyone if irrefutable proof were ever un-
covered that they made it. In hopes of making just such a
discovery, Simo is already planning an expedition for the spring
of 2001 to look for Irvine and the camera. I'm not going to go
along—it's time for me to get back to what I care most about,
which is new routes on difficult mountains in the remote ranges.

Since the expedition, I've spent a lot of time analyzing
what we found last May, both at the site where we discovered
Mallory's body and in my effort to free-climb the Second Step.
Two questions are paramount. How did Mallory die—what
caused the accident? And did he and Irvine reach the summit?
Thanks to our success last spring, we're in a position to offer
fuller answers to both questions than any investigation in the
last seventy-five years.

One prominent factor in the equation is gear. Since the 1920s there have been many waves of innovation and improvement in mountaineering equipment. What I've tried to do is imagine, from my firsthand experience on the north face and northeast ridge, what it would have been like to be there with the equipment Mallory and Irvine had in 1924.

I think the most important piece of equipment would have been crampons. The 1924 team had crampons, but they never used them above the North Col. In an appendix in *The Fight for Everest*, called "The Organization of the Expedition," Howard Somervell wrote, "*Crampons.*—These are useful, and in May 1924 were indispensable between Camps II and III, and desirable from III to IV. They are useless higher." It's odd that he should have used the word "useless"—time and again above Camp IV, crampons would have saved the men huge amounts of time on ground where they had had to chop steps. We know from Irvine's diary and from other stray remarks that the real problem was that the crampon straps cut off circulation to the feet in the soft leather boots the men wore. Above the North Col, crampons were an invitation to serious frostbite.

They did have hobnails on their boots. Mallory's right boot, which Andy and Thom retrieved, had tiny V-shaped metal wedges imbedded in the sole, sticking out maybe a quarter of an inch. I've never worn hobnailed boots, and I'd like to try out a pair on the kind of terrain Mallory and Irvine crossed up high. My guess, though, is that hobnails could give a good purchase on the shaley rock on Everest, and that you'd get a little more traction on snow than you get in a modern pair of heavy mountain boots with rubber soles, but that on hard ice you wouldn't get a proper bite. Mallory was extremely fast and skillful at chopping steps, but the best step-chopper in the world is going to go many times slower, and use much more energy, than a guy just stomping up the ice in modern crampons. I never took my crampons off throughout the whole summit day. They're not as good as rubber soles on rock, but they're so much better on ice and snow that the trade-off was well worth it.

Another very important difference between now and 1924 is fixed ropes, which offer several advantages to modern climbers. First, they indicate where the route goes. To find our way through the Yellow Band in the predawn darkness on May

17, we simply looked for the fixed ropes. Mallory and Irvine, instead, would have had to route-find on their own, both up and down.

Second, a fixed rope makes a huge difference in support. You can just wrap it around your arm, give it a tug every other step or so, or slide down it on the descent. It's like the difference between riding a subway standing in a moving car and standing there holding the subway strap. On the steepest sections, like the three Steps on the summit ridge, we rappelled fixed lines to get down. That's infinitely easier and safer than down-climbing those pitches.

The improvement in technical gear since 1924 has been astronomical. Mallory and Irvine were tied together with a cotton rope about three eighths of an inch in diameter or less. It's hard to calculate, but with knots tied in the rope, and if it was wet, the breaking strength might have been as little as 500 pounds. The breaking strength of the relatively light nylon rope I led the Second Step with was over 3,500 pounds. Also, nylon stretches to absorb impact, but cotton doesn't. In the two previous accidents in Mallory's career that were very close calls, it was something of a miracle that the rope didn't break. On the Nesthorn in 1909, when he fell forty feet free, Geoffrey Winthrop Young expected the rope to break. And when Mallory held his three falling comrades on the snow slope in 1922 with his extraordinary ice axe belay, as he later wrote of such predicaments, "In ninety-nine cases out of a hundred either the belay will give or the rope will break."

On the Continent in the 1920s, climbers were using pitons to protect their leads, but not in Britain, where for decades thereafter purists sneered at what they called "ironmongery." There is no evidence that the 1924 expedition had any metal pitons, piton hammers, or even carabiners among their gear. (Unfortunately, in *The Fight for Everest* no equipment list was published.) The book mentions "wooden pitons" being used to fix ropes below the North Col, but as there is no rock on the East Rongbuk there, my guess is that what they were using were long pickets made of wood. These would have been of no use up high.

All this means that the Second Step would have been an utterly terrifying proposition in 1924. Irvine would have had to stand belaying at the base of the final cliff, unanchored to the mountain. Had Mallory fallen anywhere while climbing up the overhanging crack, both men would most likely have been ripped off the Step and flung headlong into a fatal fall.

We know from Mallory's note that he forgot his compass at Camp V. That probably didn't matter so much, unless they were caught in a whiteout, but Odell's description of the weather on June 8 makes that sound improbable. And we know from the 1933 discovery of Mallory's flashlight in Camp VI that he forgot that too on his summit day. Most likely he also forgot to take the magnesium flares to be used in an emergency, for Odell saw one or two of them in the tent at VI. The absence of the flashlight could have had serious consequences if the two men were descending in the dark.

In 1924, not only were the oxygen cylinders leaky, the whole apparatus flawed (to Irvine's constant despair), but the rig was much heavier than what we carried. Our outfit weighed fourteen pounds, Mallory's over thirty. In that last note to Odell, he comments on the burden—"it's a bloody load for climbing." That weight would have slowed down the fittest climber. In addition, each of our bottles gave two to three times as much oxygen as the 1924 cylinders.

Finally, in terms of clothing: Mallory had on leather single boots, two pairs of stockings Ruth had knitted for him, long underwear, knickers, and puttees—picture an Ace bandage wrapped around the ankle and calf to keep out snow. On his upper body, he had seven or eight layers of silk, cotton, and wool. On his head, what looked like a pilot's cap with a fur lining.

In contrast, the day I went for the top I had on two layers of fleece, a synthethic wind parka, and a full down suit with a wind-resistant surface. On my head, a knit hat and the built-in down hood on my jacket. On my feet, thick nylon boots insulated with closed-cell foam, with gaiters built in to keep snow out of the ankles. The suit alone provides three to four inches of insulation, which is a lot more than all seven or eight of Mallory's layers combined. Yet even with my snazzy state-of-the-art clothing, I'd get very cold when I had to stop and wait for any length of time.

Another important consideration is how well hydrated

Mallory and Irvine were when they set out on June 8. We know from Mallory's note to Odell that "our Unna Cooker rolled down the slope at the last moment." The latest that note could have been written was the afternoon of June 7, because the Sherpas carried the note down to Camp V that day. Unless Mallory and Irvine had heated snow to fill their Thermoses with water for the climb the next day even before cooking dinner, the loss of the stove would have meant they had no water and couldn't properly hydrate. They might have tried to fill the Thermoses with snow and melt it with body heat in the night, but that's a desperate emergency measure. On Annapurna IV I was stuck in a snow cave for five days and tried that technique with a water bottle. It was horrid: I filled the bottle with snow and kept it between my legs all evening, but managed to melt only a cupful of water. The procedure costs you more in heat loss than you gain in energy from the liquid.

So if they set out on the morning of June 8 already dehydrated, that would have taken a drastic toll. On top of this, Irvine was terribly sunburned, and sunburn dehydrates you further.

Another argument against their having made the summit has to do with rates of ascent. I'm convinced that the fact that Mallory forgot his flashlight indicates that they set out at or after sunrise. You don't forget your flashlight if you leave while it's still dark. So far as I can determine, nobody in either 1922 or 1924 ever got off from a high camp before 6:30 in the morning. By contrast the six of us set out at 2:30 A.M. on May 17.

In *First on Everest: The Mystery of Mallory & Irvine*, Tom Holzel calculates a theoretical rate of ascent for the two men of 204 vertical feet per hour. This forms a crucial part of his argument that Mallory could have made the top. It took Dave and me twelve hours and twenty minutes to go from Camp VI to the summit. That's averaging only 165 vertical feet per hour. Dave and I are relatively rapid climbers, he'd been to the top before, and we had the tremendous advantage over Mallory and Irvine of crampons and fixed ropes. I find it hard to believe they could have climbed significantly faster than we did along the northeast ridge.

All of these considerations add up to a strong case in my mind that Mallory and Irvine did not summit on June 8, 1924. But the clincher for me is the Second Step.

First of all, it's worth pointing out that on the northeast ridge, there's no alternative to climbing the Second Step where the Chinese tied their ladder. On the prow of the ridge, the rock is completely rotten and vertical. On the left, over the Kang-shung Face, there's just snow with the consistency of whipped cream plastered onto very steep ice. It's probably unclimbable today, even with ice tools and crampon front-points, and there was certainly no hope of climbing it in 1924 in the traditional style of chopping steps. To the right of the ladder, the rock just gets steeper and steeper. You could traverse far beneath the ridge and get into the Great Couloir, as Norton did on June 4, and so avoid the Second Step. But once you're above the Yellow Band, to traverse into the Great Couloir could actually be more difficult and demanding than to climb the Second Step.

Let's imagine that Mallory and Irvine could have gotten up the bottom half of the Second Step. I'd rate the moves there as about 5.5, which Mallory could have done. But then Irvine would have had to stand at the top of the snow triangle, where Dave tied in to the ladder, and try to get some sort of stance without an anchor. He would have belayed Mallory with that flimsy cotton rope wrapped around his waist, exactly as Geof-frey Winthrop Young belayed Mallory on the Nesthorn. Mal-lory would have had to climb the slightly overhanging fifteen-foot crack without a single piece of protection. The cam I was able to place under the chockstone some fifteen feet up was the only possible protection, and that type of gear wasn't in-vented until the late 1970s.

Even with a secure belay, a cam for protection, a good nylon rope, and a rest on the ladder rung I stepped on, I found the pitch desperately hard. By the 1920s, a few climbs as hard as 5.10 on lowland European crags like the Elbsandsteingebirge near Dresden had been done, by wizards way ahead of their time, using pitons or ring bolts or rope loops tied through holes in the rocks. But not by Britons in Wales: at the time, the hard-est pitches in Great Britain were probably at the 5.7 to 5.8 level. That sort of pitch is an entirely different proposition at 28,230 feet on Everest.

Incidentally, I'm convinced—as Reinhold Messner is too—that the Chinese did not climb the Second Step in 1960. It's un-fathomable to think of taking off your boots and trying the cliff in stocking feet there. It's too convenient that reaching the top in the dark explains the team's failure to bring back summit photos. And I suspect that reporting the crux of the cliff at the Second Step as only three meters high, when in truth it's a good twenty-five feet, was a concoction to make it plausible that it could have been surmounted by a shoulder stand.

Even if Mallory and Irvine had miraculously climbed the Second Step, they would have been stranded above it. Few climbing ropes at the time were longer than 100 feet. Had they doubled the rope around the anchoring boulder at the top and rappelled the Step, the rope would never have reached. Nor would they have been able to pull the rope down from below, because the boulder sits so far back on the shelf that the friction would have been prohibitive. An alternative would have been to tie the rope to the boulder, rappel it single-strand, and leave the rope there. But no one since has ever found any trace of an anchor or a rope from 1924 above the Second Step.

Even if I had successfully free-climbed the Step, there's no way I could have down-climbed it. Some people have wondered whether Mallory and Irvine might have fallen to their deaths trying to do just that. But if they'd come off there, they would have fallen all the way to the Rongbuk Glacier.

There's one possible loophole in this matter. If 1924 was an unusually heavy year for snow, it's conceivable that a snow cone could have drifted in, covering the vertical cliffs of the Second Step, in which case Mallory and Irvine could have just walked up the cone. During May that year, the expedition was hit by one storm after another. But on the north face, snow doesn't stay long—it tends to get quickly blown off. In the few photos I've seen from 1924, even from far below you can see the thin black band of the upper Second Step. The only expedition in recent years to report anything like a snow cone here was that of the Catalans in 1985, but they came to Everest in the autumn season, after the monsoon. Even they had to climb the top four or five rungs of the ladder.

In my heart, I've always wanted to believe Mallory and Irvine could have climbed the mountain in 1924. It would have made for one of the ultimate of all mountaineering tales. It makes me sad to be on the skeptical, debunking side of the debate, but for all the reasons I've laid out above, I believe there is no possible way Mallory and Irvine could have reached the summit.

WHAT DO I THINK happened, then, on June 8, 1924?

Imagine Mallory and Irvine at Camp VI that morning, looking toward the summit. For Mallory, this was the mountain of his dreams. He was the only man who'd tried Everest on three expeditions; now, after a month of defeat, he had one last chance. He had the resources and the weather to give it a good shot.

But the pair of men were tired from the tough two-day climb up from the North Col. Irvine had terrible sunburn, his lips cracked, pieces of his skin peeling off whenever his face rubbed against anything. Probably their eyes were sore, from the grit and sun—even with modern goggles, I pick up that irritation at high altitude. By evening, my eyes are red and feel very scratchy. The sun adds a significant debilitating factor to any effort at altitude, one too often underestimated.

It's possible they used oxygen to sleep, but I'd guess they saved it for the climb. Without oxygen, it's difficult to sleep at that altitude. You develop a cyclic breathing pattern—fast and shallow breaths alternating with no breaths at all—which wakes you up again and again. It's an autonomic reaction of the body to lack of oxygen. So I'd guess they went to bed early, but just tossed and turned most of the night.

And maybe in the morning, Irvine made desperate last-minute repairs to the oxygen apparatus. I don't buy Odell's notion that he might have just been puttering, "invent[ing] some problem to be solved even if it never really had turned up." Oxygen problems could have delayed their getting off in the morning. And again, it seems certain that it was light when they left, because Mallory forgot his flashlight.

They headed up using oxygen, probably two bottles per man, maybe at a flow of about two liters per minute. They climbed through the Yellow Band, which in itself is trying, difficult terrain. Tom Holzel argues that a bottle would have lasted them a little more than four hours, but I don't think you can be that precise, so many things can go wrong at altitude. In any event, they discarded a bottle between the top of the Yellow Band and the First Step, where Tap and Jake found it this year.

Even with oxygen, altitude confuses your sense of time.

You think you've been doing something for fifteen minutes, but you've been doing it for an hour. A metaphor occurred to me after my experience this year on Everest. At altitude, it's as if there's a house burning, and the house that's burning is you, but everything's happening at such a dragged-out pace you can't do anything about it. You just watch the house burn down.

Mallory and Irvine may have been taking four or five breaths for each step. Or they may have taken as many as four-teen or fifteen—that's not uncommon among modern climbers, even with oxygen. No matter what, I'm sure their pace was slower than Mallory had hoped. They made the long diagonal traverse from the top of the Yellow Band to the First Step. I'm convinced they climbed the First Step, and that somewhere near there is where Odell saw them at 12:50. But then they faced the tricky traverse from the First Step to the Second. It would have been amazing to have climbed this in 1924, and it would mean that they'd gotten about a hundred feet higher than Norton had four days before. That in turn means that nobody got higher on the surface of the earth for the next twenty-eight years.

But somewhere on that traverse, they recognized that it wasn't in the cards, that they weren't going to make it to the top. If they'd had an exceptional climbing day, and everything had gone right, they might have reached the foot of the Second Step. But they turned back. Now the snow squall that Odell re-ported blew in. The new snow would have filled their tracks, meaning that they had to try to find the route all over again on the way down. The tricky part even today is finding the exit cracks at the top of the Yellow Band.

My guess is that Mallory was going first: he wouldn't have left the route-finding up to Irvine. And just as I started to do with Dave, he started down the Yellow Band too early, too far west. At some point in the afternoon, the weather cleared up again, and Odell looked for his friends, but if they were in the rocks of the Yellow Band as opposed to outlined against the sky, there was little chance he could spot them.

We know that Mallory and Irvine were roped together. At the time, a common practice on moderate mixed ground was to travel roped together, with the second man carrying coils. It turns out to be an incredibly dangerous practice—the very chore of managing the rope and maintaining a steady distance between climbers can cause accidents, and the chance of one man's belaying and stopping the other's fall is slim at best. Yet as late as the 1960s, mountaineers were still teaching this technique.

There are many places where you can climb through the Yellow Band. Much of it lies at that tricky angle where you're torn between down-climbing and rappelling. The rocks are all downsloping and loose. Mallory would have been intensely focused here. And I'd guess that either it was approaching dusk or the men were descending in the squall, so he took off his goggles to see the rock better. They would have been moving together on the easier parts, maybe stopping to give a little belay on the harder stretches—the rope hooked over a prong or corner, like the "nick" Geoffrey Winthrop Young used to belay Mallory on the Nesthorn.

Since May 1, I've thought a lot about Mallory's hands. Why wasn't he wearing gloves? He had the spare pair of fingerless knit gloves in his pocket, but they looked as though they'd never been used. The other thing that struck me at once is that the hands showed no signs of frostbite.

A number of people, especially those who would like to believe Mallory and Irvine made the summit, have hypothesized that they spent the night of June 8 in an open bivouac, then fell descending on the ninth. But with their clothing, there would have been no way to spend a night out above 27,000 feet and not suffer serious frostbite. When your fingers freeze, they develop "blebs," puffy blisters, although it takes them from twenty-four to forty-eight hours to swell up. Mallory's fingers showed no sign of blebs. On May 16 this year, during the second search, Thom Pollard had dug up Mallory's face. I asked him if there was any sign of frostbite; he said no. Unlike the fingers, the nose and cheeks react right away to frostbite, turning first white and gray, then black.

The absence of frostbite on Mallory's mummified body proves to me that he died on June 8, not the next day. As the blood ceases to flow upon death, a deceased person doesn't develop frostbite.

My hunch is that when he fell, Mallory had taken off his gloves so that he could face inward and grasp the rocks better. Maybe it was dark by then, and down-climbing in the dark, with no flashlight, would have been all but impossible.

Everyone has wondered whether one man fell and pulled the other off, or if Irvine belayed Mallory's fall and the rope broke over an edge. In the latter case, Irvine would have been left to try to descend alone in the dark. This scenario might fit well with Wang Hongbao's "old English dead"—maybe the Chinese climber in 1975 found Irvine where he had tried to wait out the night and had frozen to death. But I doubt it, for one good reason. If Irvine had belayed Mallory and the rope had broken when Mallory's weight came on it, the rope would have parted near Irvine's end. Instead, we found it broken only some ten feet away from Mallory's waist.

I think, then, that one man pulled the other off (it could have been Irvine, coming second, who fell), that both men plunged down the mountain together, and that the rope sawed over a rock edge. That's happened often over the years, even with good nylon ropes. And if I'm right, the place to look for Irvine is not in Hemmleb's search zone, which is up and left, or east, of where I found Mallory, but rather to the right or west of Mallory, because when the accident happened they would have been diagonaling down and eastward with Mallory in the lead.

In my scenario, as Mallory fell, the rope tangled around him. The initial impact came on his right side. It's significant too that it was his right leg that was so badly broken. It was his right ankle that he'd broken in 1909, and on Everest in 1924, it was his right leg, from the ankle up to the hip, that was still giving him trouble. No doubt the initial break had permanently weakened the leg.

I'm also quite sure that Mallory didn't fall from all the way up on the northeast ridge—say from where the ice axe was found in 1933. The two modern bodies I found just before I discovered Mallory—the Greeter, and the guy in the faded blue suit—were so much more broken up, their limbs sprawled every which way, their heads downhill. Those two had fallen from the ridge, I'd venture. But Mallory's body wasn't so contorted, and his head was uphill. I'd guess he fell only some 300 to 400 vertical feet, which would mean he came off near the bottom of the Yellow Band. Even in the dark, he might have been close to pulling off a successful retreat.

Was he still alive when he came to rest? It's hard to say. The hole in his forehead that Thom discovered may have been the injury that killed him. But the hands planted in the scree looked like those of a man still trying to self-arrest with his fingers. I think he was fighting to the very end.

The position of his legs suggests he set them that way to relieve the pain. If so, his synapses were still firing, and before he lapsed into unconsciousness he may have thought for a moment that he and Irvine could have made it to camp safely. Quickly and silently shock set in, as Mallory became one with the Mother Goddess of the Snows.

MY BELIEF that Mallory could not have reached the summit does nothing to diminish my fascination with the man.

Last spring, I embarked on our expedition with summitting Everest as my primary goal. I felt that a grand opportunity had presented itself, even though many of my climbing peers and I were doubtful that we'd find anything. A high school friend had chuckled, "Sounds like you've landed a big fish." A chance to go to Everest, he meant, with no costs attached. A bit defensively, I answered, "You never know what you might find, especially in a static environment like the high Himalaya."

All my feelings changed on May 1. As I discovered the body of George Mallory, I realized we had reopened a chapter in our climbing heritage. Sitting next to Mallory gave me a deep appreciation for what he'd done and stood for.

Alone with Sandy Irvine, after the sun had set, on the immense north face of Everest, the nearest other teammate 4,000 feet below with no possible knowledge where the two men were, or that they needed help—that in itself was a remarkable place to have arrived. The whole journey had been an epic voyage: by steamer from Liverpool to Bombay, overland by train to Darjeeling, across the Himalayan crest on pony-back to the little-known regions of Tibet, over remote passes into unexplored valleys. Thus the climbers ventured to crack the puzzle of what had come to be called the Third Pole. With them they hauled vast stores of equipment—cutting-edge gear for the day, utterly rudimentary by our standards.

The mystery of altitude itself had scarcely been probed. To know, as we do today, that Everest has been climbed solo and without bottled oxygen makes the challenge less intimidating. Even with the knowledge Mallory had gained about altitude in

1921 and '22, it remained an unsolved question whether it was humanly possible to climb to 29,000 feet and survive. Each step the climbers took above Camp VI in 1924 was a step into the terra incognita of the mind.

Sitting beside Mallory on May 1, I looked east toward the descent route he and Irvine would have taken had they summitted that June 8. I imagined Mallory's awareness even in extremis: no radio to communicate with others, no chain of fixed ropes to guide him down the mountain, no teams of rested climbers ready to enact a rescue, no way of telling the world what really happened.

I can only guess what Mallory's and Irvine's last moments were like, but what I do know is how their achievement has affected our climbing legacy. The boldness of their last climb formed a stepping-stone to the future. The debate over oxygen and its ultimate acceptance made it possible for their successors—including Hillary and Tenzing—to visit high places with a reasonable safety margin.

Sometimes late at night I wonder whether by discovering Mallory I've aided in the destruction of a mystery. The possibility haunts me. Has my find somehow taken some of the enigmatic glory away from the 1924 expedition?

Others may think so, yet for me, the discovery only increases my admiration for these pioneer climbers, whose story—which will never be told in its entirety—has always lain wrapped in the secrets of Chomolungma, Mother Goddess of the Snows. I feel privileged to have participated in casting new light onto this mystery. Ultimately, Mallory and Irvine's greatest achievement was an inspirational one, for even in failure, their magnificent attempt showed us what the human spirit is capable of.

As the surviving members of the 1924 expedition retreated from the mountain, they engaged in long conversations about what must have happened to their vanished friends. Even before they had left Base Camp, Teddy Norton convened a conference to discuss the matter. Every member but Odell concurred in thinking that the most likely course of events had been what indeed we now know happened: "a simple mountaineering accident—a slip and sudden death." Odell adamantly held out for the view that the two men had delayed their return until it was too late, then had "wandered about in the darkness looking for [Camp VI] until they finally succumbed to exhaustion and exposure."

Odell simply could not believe that Mallory would have fallen. As he wrote in *The Fight for Everest*, "It is difficult for any who knew the skill and experience of George Mallory on all kinds and conditions of mountain ground to believe that he fell, and where the difficulties to him would be so insignificant." As for Irvine, he was "a natural adept"; in Spitsbergen, he had proven "able to move safely and easily on rock and ice."

Their teammates puzzled incessantly over why they had seen no beam from a flashlight the night of June 8, but not until 1933 would they learn that Mallory had left his flashlight in the tent at Camp VI. Sir Francis Younghusband, in *The Epic of Mount Everest*, went so far as to surmise that, in a hopeless predicament, Mallory and Irvine might have refused to shine their flashlight out of a sense of "chivalry," lest they draw their teammates into unnecessary danger trying to rescue them.

Norton claimed that he and Mallory had agreed on a turn-around deadline of 4:00 P.M. Odell found it hard to reconcile his theory of benightment with this evidence of Mallory's prudence, but concluded that his friend's "craving for victory" had become an obsession that "may have been too strong for him." John Noel likewise speculated, in his memoir, *The Story of Everest*:

> You can imagine how Mallory's energy of nerve, brain and muscle must have risen to the supreme effort of his life. . . . The goal was in their grasp. Should they turn back and lose it? . . . Might they not indeed throw every other thought to the wind to win such a prize?

On a moraine heap near Base Camp, Somervell and several porters built a ten-foot-high cairn memorializing the dead of all three Everest expeditions, with their names carved into smooth slabs. From Base, Norton sent a runner off with a coded message to be cabled to London: "MALLORY IRVINE NOVE REMAINDER ALCEDO."

This message, which has never been publicly explicated, appears to have used code words linked to possible events—just like the 1999 team's "gorak" for "camera" and "boulder" for "body." In 1924, the code words may have had Latin associations. "Nove" means "new" or "fresh"; in the superlative, "novissime" means "in the last place." "Alcedo" refers to the kingfisher and, more specifically, to "the fourteen days in winter, when the kingfisher lays its eggs and the sea is calm."

On the original telegram, received in London on June 19, someone has penciled "killed in last engagement" next to "NOVE," and "arrived base all in good order" next to "ALCEDO."

According to biographer David Robertson, "Ruth received the news in Cambridge from a representative of the press. She went out for a long walk with old friends."

At eighty-three, Clare Millikan remembers precisely how she learned of her father's death when she was eight. "It was getting-up time," she says. "Mother took us into her bedroom. We all lay in bed together, with her arms around us. Then she told us. There was nothing confusing about it. He wasn't 'missing'—he was quite definitely dead. He wasn't coming back."

The whole country went into mourning. Fifty-nine years earlier, in the most famous mountaineering accident before Mallory and Irvine's, when four men, including the aristocrat Lord Francis Douglas, lost their lives in a long fall coming down from the first ascent of the Matterhorn, Queen Victoria had condemned the pastime. But in the interim, England had turned its lost explorers Robert Falcon Scott and his four companions, who had died in 1912 on their return from the South Pole, into martyr-heroes. Now King George V sent his deepest sympathies to the families of Mallory and Irvine. Endorsing the nation's pride in its brave dead, the *Morning Post* editorialized, "The spirit which animated the attacks on Everest is the same as that which prompted arctic and other expeditions, and in earlier times led to the formation of the Empire itself."

On October 17, a memorial service for the two men was

held in St. Paul's Cathedral. That evening, at a joint meeting of the Alpine Club and the Royal Geographical Society, Norton said of Mallory, "A fire burnt in him. . . . He was absolutely determined to conquer the mountain. . . . His death leaves us poorer by a loyal friend, a great mountaineer, and a gallant gentleman." Mallory's mentor, Geoffrey Winthrop Young, spoke in his obituary of the man's "burning spirit of chivalrous, youthful adventure, flaming at the close." In Young's recollection, Mallory had been " 'Sir Galahad' always to his early friends." In the expedition book, Geoffrey Bruce called him "the Bayard of the Mountains—*'sans peur et sans reproche'* [fearless and beyond reproach]." Wrote Howard Somervell in *After Everest:*

> *Dulce et decorum est pro patria mori;* and surely death in battle against a mountain is a finer and nobler thing than death whilst attempting to kill someone else. The loss of these splendid men is part of the price that has been paid to keep alive the spirit of adventure. Without this spirit life would be a poor thing, and progress impossible.

Hand in hand with this apotheosis of Mallory and Irvine came the sentiment that Everest was a fitting place to die, "the finest cenotaph in the world," in Somervell's phrase. Sir Francis Younghusband made the observation, in *The Epic of Mount Everest,* that "there in the arms of Mount Everest they lie for ever—lie 10,000 feet above where any man has lain in death before." Younghusband's altitude was exaggerated—the Sherpas killed below the North Col in 1922 lay at that moment entombed in ice only 4,000 feet below Mallory's body—but the thought was at once a startling and an enthralling one.

From the moment the news broke in England, the great question of whether Mallory and Irvine had reached the summit preoccupied all who took notice of the tragedy. Noel Odell believed that his friends had climbed Everest: as he wrote in the London *Times* on July 10, "Considering all the circumstances and the position they had reached on the mountain, I personally am of [the] opinion that Mallory and Irvine must have reached the summit." General Charles Bruce agreed, as did Tom Longstaff and Geoffrey Winthrop Young. Wrote the latter,

"After nearly 20 years' knowledge of Mallory as a mountaineer, I can say . . . that difficult as it would have been for any mountaineer to turn back with the only difficulty past—to Mallory it would have been an impossibility."

These men, of course, were swayed by their friendship with Mallory and admiration of his drive. The members of the 1933 expedition—perhaps for the opposite reason, for they had not ventured to Tibet to make the *second* ascent of Everest— were convinced to a man that Mallory and Irvine had not reached the top.

Beneath the public outpouring of admiration and sorrow, Mallory's closest friends sorely missed him. Trying to strike a bluff tone, Robert Graves wrote Ruth: "My only consolation is that he once told me on Snowdon that he'd hoped to die like that, climbing. . . . So like George to choose the highest and most dangerous mountain in the world! I did love him."

A month after she had learned the news, still beside herself with grief, Ruth wrote to Geoffrey Winthrop Young,

> Whether he got to the top of the mountain or did not, whether he lived or died, makes no difference to my admiration for him. I think I have got the pain separate. There is so much of it, and it will go on so long, that I must do that. . . .
> Oh Geoffrey, if only it hadn't happened! It so easily might not have.

Sometime in the first weeks after losing her father, Clare Millikan had a vivid dream. "When I was young," she recalls, "during the war, he'd always come and gone a lot from the front in France. I would look over an embankment, see his train, see him coming toward us.

"In my dream, I looked over the embankment, saw the train, saw him get out and walk toward us. It was a very painful awakening."

Seventy-five years after his fatal fall, the legend of George Leigh Mallory shows no signs of dimming. Whether or not he reached the summit, there is no denying that the man was a genius of ascent, and that Everest brought out the finest in him. The friends who knew him best kept coming back to that talismanic fact. For Geoffrey Winthrop Young, grieving the loss of his protégé, the summit must have been reached, in the final analysis, simply "because Mallory was Mallory." And a quarter-century after his disappearance, Young remembered a blithe route the pair had climbed in Wales: "The laughing hours chased each other unnoticed. . . . On a day like this, and in movement, Mallory was wholly in harmony within himself, and with the world, and nothing could give him pause."

Acknowledgments

DR

THE WORK of previous scholars on Mallory and Everest has been invaluable to us in researching *The Lost Explorer*. In particular, Audrey Salkeld and Tom Holzel's *First on Everest: The Mystery of Mallory & Irvine* offers a deft synthesis of character and climbing deeds; David Pye's *George Leigh Mallory: A Memoir* benefits from Pye's friendship with his subject; David Robertson's definitive biography, *George Mallory*, is rich in quotations from the private letters; Herbert Carr's *The Irvine Diaries* affords a closer look at Mallory's partner, so often relegated to the shadows; and Walt Unsworth's comprehensive *Everest* is a gold mine of information for all the expeditions to the mountain between 1921 and 1988. The three massive official expedition books from the 1920s—*Mount Everest: The Reconnaissance, 1921; The Assault on Mount Everest, 1922;* and *The Fight for Everest*—are irreplaceable. The library of the American Alpine Club in Golden, Colorado, lent me these classic tomes, and served as a welcome repository for other scholarly materials I would have been hard put to find elsewhere.

To the members of the 1999 Mallory & Irvine Research Expedition, as well as to Liesl Clark of PBS/*NOVA* and Peter Potterfield of MountainZone, we owe a special debt for sharing their knowledge and their experiences on the mountain last spring. Kathmandu mountaineering historian Elizabeth Hawley filled in details no one else seemed to have at hand.

I feel a lasting gratitude to my editor and longtime friend

John Rasmus, who assigned me a story about finding Mallory for *National Geographic Adventure*, which led indirectly to this book. Rasmus's colleagues at the magazine were a great help throughout. Jon Krakauer read each chapter in draft and gave us superb advice and constant encouragement. David Breashears and Galen Rowell lent their support and expertise, based on their own vast experience on Everest. Agent John Ware shepherded the project from start to finish with consummate skill. And my editor at Simon & Schuster, Bob Bender—my loyal cicerone through four books now—made *The Lost Explorer* happen, not without the perspicacious aid of his assistant, Johanna Li.

Finally, I feel a warm appreciation for Clare, Rick, and George Millikan, friends and climbing partners since the early 1960s, through whose unique connection to the hero of this book I first began to know George Mallory.

I WOULD LIKE TO THANK my parents for their many years of support for and encouragement of this life I lead; and Dave Hahn, for the invitation to join this journey of discovery to the highest point on earth.

TO ALEX LOWE AND SETH SHAW, who lost their lives in the high mountains, I will always be inspired by you. Alex, for your unconditional love of your family, and Seth, for your modesty, intelligence, and strength. I love you both.

Index

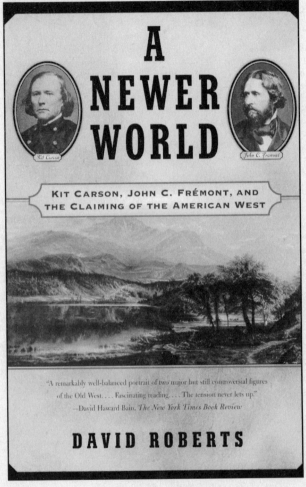